VEGETARIAN
WOK
COOKING

by Marlisa Szwillus

Illustrated with photographs by Heinz-Josef Beckers

Translated from the German by Elizabeth D. Crawford

BARRON'S

TABLE OF CONTENTS

The Wok—An All-Purpose Utensil

The wok, probably the world's most ingenious universal cooking utensil, was invented in China centuries ago. Originally the iron pan with its curving bottom was designed for open fires; later it was used for stoves with a fire hole. The secret of the wok, its deep and almost semicircular form, arose out of necessity. Food and fuel were always in very short supply in China. To use both to the best advantage, the Chinese cut the few ingredients into very small pieces. So on the one hand they required only a short cooking time and thus little firewood, and on the other hand the dishes appeared to be more voluminous.

Now as ever, the wok plays a leading role in Asian cuisine because it can be used for frying, braising, steaming, deep-frying, blanching, and even smoking. But modern Western kitchens are also incomplete without the multitalented pot. It is even well suited for use as a fondue pot for a congenial circle of guests. In principle, nothing is simpler than cooking in a wok.

Enjoyment and Well-Being

Asian cooking keeps winning new friends in the West, and for good reason: Everyone gets his money's worth in enjoyment, the variety is fascinating, the dishes look colorful and appetizing, and the large proportion of vegetarian dishes corresponds to our steadily growing demand for a healthy and conscientious choice of foods.

The wok is inseparably bound to Far Eastern cooking, but any dishes you would otherwise cook in a saucepan or frying pan succeed superbly in the wok. Many American and international dishes can be prepared even more simply and nutritiously in this all-around pot.

Modern Woks

Unlike Asia, kitchens here are furnished with gas or electric stoves so most Western woks have flat and smooth rather than curved bottoms. For cooking on a gas stove, a special ring stand steadies the wok and holds it the right distance from the flame.

Woks are available in many different materials and models; the choice is ultimately a question of price. Some woks are coated to prevent the food from sticking. A wok should heat up fast and distribute the heat evenly. These characteristics are guaranteed by cast iron, enameled cast iron, stainless steel, or copper. A high, curved cover is a must; you need it for braising, steaming, and keeping the dish warm. So-called party woks—which function as wok, fondue pot, and grill combined—are heated by electricity or gas or furnished with a heat source and burner. You can also fry right at the table with these.

The Larger the Better

To prepare four servings you need a wok at least 12 to 14 in (30 to 35 cm) in diameter. With this size you have enough room to distribute the ingredients so that all can cook evenly. In smaller woks, with a diameter of 10 to 11 in (25 to 28 cm), you can only cook one or two servings adequately; for a larger quantity, you should always prepare the dish in two batches. When you buy a new wok, it's better to choose a larger one, for it will also be ideal for smaller quantities.

Use and Care

Before the first use, wash out the wok with hot water and some detergent, dry it, oil it well, and heat it briefly. Always follow the directions for use that come with the wok. For instance, cast iron woks must be rubbed with oil after each use so that no rust can get started. Woks with nonstick coatings and those of stainless steel are easier to care for; just washing is enough for these.

Useful Accessories

Most woks are sold with accessories. But you can also buy the parts individually in housewares stores or Asian shops.

Semicircular draining rack: This is suspended from the edge of the wok to steam small quantities, keep food warm, or let deep-fried foods drain.

Spatula with rounded front edge: Its rounded edge fits the curve of the wok so the ingredients can be easily lifted and turned.

Slotted ladle: Ideal for lifting large pieces from a sauce or fried foods from fat.

Sieve insert or steamer basket: A practical necessity for steaming to preserve nutrients. May be made of metal or bamboo.

Rustled Up
in a $\mathcal{F}$lash

Stir-Frying

This is the term for frying in the wok. It is a typical Asian cooking method in which the requirements are speed and constant control. First the dry wok is heated, and only then do you add a small amount of fat and fry the ingredients in it over high heat while stirring constantly. In the process of stirring, the ingredients come into contact with the very hot bottom and the hot wok walls in rapid succession and thus cook evenly and very fast.

Organization Is Everything

During the frying, which rarely takes longer than 5 to 10 minutes, you are constantly busy with stirring and turning and have no time for anything else. Therefore you must be entirely prepared ahead of time: ingredients cut small, seasonings ready, and liquids measured. The side dishes should also be prepared ahead of time.

Preparation of the Wok

The wok must be hot enough so that the outer surfaces of the ingredients will be seared as fast as possible and no juices can leak out. Therefore, heat the empty wok first. You can establish with the water-drop test whether it is hot enough: Spray a few drops of water on the bottom of the wok. If they hiss, it isn't hot enough yet. But if they form little "dancing" balls of water, the right moment has arrived. Then carefully oil the wok with cooking oil on a paper towel or a brush, so that later nothing can "hang up" on the bottom or the walls. Only now add the real frying oil and heat it until just under the smoking point.

Stirring in the Wok

In frying, always begin with the one or several ingredients that take the longest to cook. Among the vegetables, these include carrots and celery root, for example. More delicate ones, such as peas and leafy greens, are added later, and watery ones like tomatoes are added at the very end. Important: Stir everything constantly from the inside to the outside. Fry the first vegetables, without browning them, and push them out to the edge of the pan in a ring to keep them warm. Then add the next ingredient, fry, mix with the first, again push all out to the edge, and so on. It is important that the quantity of vegetables in the wok be just large enough that the pieces lie next to each other and not on top of each other; otherwise they will steam rather than fry. With a smaller wok or a larger quantity, always fry in batches; take out each batch and keep it warm. At the end, stir all the ingredients together in the wok again, mix with some liquid if required, and season. Done!

Healthy and Delicious

The short cooking time preserves everything that is so prized in fresh vegetables: flavor, color, and crisp consistency. Vitamins and minerals are preserved, and you manage with a minimum of fat. Fast cooking gives vegetables an entirely different taste: The starch in them changes into sugar and caramelizes. This is particularly noticeable with onions and carrots.

Tips for Frying in the Wok

• For stir-frying, if nothing else is listed in the recipe, preferably use a highly heatable fat like taste-neutral sunflower seed, corn, or soy oil. Or use peanut oil or clarified butter. Cold-pressed oils are unsuitable for these high temperatures.

• For stir-frying on an electric stove, because of the slower response to heat regulation, it is a good idea to work on two burners—one with a higher temperature and one with a lower one. This way you can quickly change and always have the right heat level.

• With stir-frying, always keep a little dish of water next to the stove. If you have the feeling, especially when frying large quantities, that the ingredients near the wok walls are drying out, sprinkle them with a tiny amount of water.

Practical Quantities

In stir-frying you often need only very small quantities of liquid to deglaze. This can be water, wine, coconut milk, prepared seasoning sauce, or vegetable broth. When you use broth, you can decide whether to use an instant broth, a vegetable base from a jar, or a homemade vegetable broth (recipe on page 27).

Homemade broth cannot be prepared in such small quantities, of course; therefore it pays to make a large amount and freeze it. A good way to fix small quantities for such purposes is to use ice cube trays. Simply fill the trays with cold broth and freeze. Thaw the required amount as needed. Not only broth, but also wine or coconut milk can be frozen in the smallest quantities in ice trays—and the cubes keep for up to six months.

Herbed Tomatoes on Millet

18 oz (500 g) millet
salt
2 lb (1 kg) meaty tomatoes
4 shallots
2 garlic cloves
4 stalks celery
1 bunch each parsley and basil
3 Tbs olive oil
¼ tsp sugar
1 Tbs balsamic vinegar
pepper
2 oz (60 g) freshly grated Parmesan cheese

Preparation time:
about 35 minutes

Scrambled Eggs with Mango

1 ripe mango
(about 18 oz/500 g)
2 scallions
8 eggs
2–3 Tbs light soy sauce
1 tsp sesame oil
2 Tbs oil
a few lettuce leaves

Preparation time:
about 20 minutes

Herbed Tomatoes on Millet

Economical • Pictured

• Let the millet come to a boil in a pot with 3 cups (24 fl oz/700 mL) water and some salt. Cook, covered, over low heat for 25 minutes.

• Meanwhile, scald the tomatoes, peel, remove the bases of the stems, and chop coarsely. Peel the shallots and garlic and mince. Clean the celery and slice thin. Wash and stem the herbs and finely chop the leaves.

• First heat the wok and then heat the oil in it. Fry the vegetables over high heat for 5 to 7 minutes, stirring constantly. Stir in the herbs, sugar, and vinegar. Season the tomatoes with salt and pepper. Serve over the millet, sprinkled with cheese.

Makes 4 servings.

Scrambled Eggs with Mango

Fast • Far-Eastern

• Peel the mango and cut the flesh from the stone in large chunks. Cut into small pieces. Trim the scallions and slice into paper-thin rings.

• Beat the eggs. Add the mango and season with soy sauce and sesame oil. Stir in the scallions.

• First heat the wok and then heat the oil in it. Pour in the egg mixture and stir over low heat until it becomes a creamy mass. Serve on the lettuce leaves with spicy dips (ready-made products) and a mixed green salad.

Makes 4 servings.

PER SERVING:	612 CALORIES	
NUTRITIONAL INFORMATION		
Fat (22% calories from fat) 15	g
Protein 22	g
Carbohydrate 98	g
Cholesterol 7	mg
Sodium 24	mg

PER SERVING:	237 CALORIES	
NUTRITIONAL INFORMATION		
Fat (51% calories from fat) 14	g
Protein 12	g
Carbohydrate 18	g
Cholesterol 361	mg
Sodium 733	mg

10 dried cloud ear mushrooms
3 Tbs light soy sauce
2 Tbs rice wine or dry sherry
3 Tbs vegetable broth or water
pinch of sugar
1 carrot
1 small red bell pepper
5 oz (150 g) Chinese (Napa) cabbage
7 oz (200 g) broccoli
7 oz (200 g) baby corn ears (fresh or bottled)
3–4 oz (100 g) snow peas
3–4 oz (100 g) button mushrooms
2 garlic cloves
1 piece fresh ginger (about ¼ in/1 cm)
34 oz (100 g) bamboo shoots
3 Tbs oil
1 Tbs sesame oil
1–2 dried chilis, crumbled
1 bunch cilantro
salt
pepper

Preparation time: about 45 minutes

Buddha Vegetables

From China • Colorful

• Cover the cloud ear mushrooms with boiling water and let soften for about 30 minutes. Meanwhile, mix the soy sauce, rice wine, vegetable broth, and sugar.

• Wash all vegetables and trim as necessary. Cut the carrot, pepper, and Chinese cabbage into strips. Divide the broccoli into the smallest possible rosettes, peel the stems, and cut into small pieces. Halve the corn ears lengthwise, string the snow peas, and quarter the button mushrooms.

• Peel the garlic and ginger and mince. Cut the bamboo shoots into fine strips. Wash the softened cloud ear mushrooms in a sieve and chop coarsely.

• First heat the wok and then heat both kinds of oil in it. Fry the garlic, ginger, and chilis in it, stirring constantly. Then stir-fry the carrot, broccoli, corn, and cloud ear mushrooms over high heat for about 3 minutes.

• Finally, fry the button mushrooms, bell pepper, snow peas, and bamboo shoots for about 2 more minutes. Add the soy sauce mixture and bring to a boil. Cook over medium heat, stirring constantly, until the vegetables are crisp-tender. Wash the cilantro, pull off the leaves, and stir in. Season the vegetables with salt and pepper. Serve with glutinous or short-grain rice.

Makes 4 servings.

Variations

• Add 5 oz (150 g) diced tofu toward the end of the cooking time.

• Substitute vegetables according to your preference. Cut them into uniformly small pieces so that they all cook in the same amount of time.

PER SERVING:	188 CALORIES	
NUTRITIONAL INFORMATION		
Fat (40% calories from fat) 8	g
Protein 7	g
Carbohydrate .20	g
Cholesterol 0	mg
Sodium 821	mg

Sweet-and-Sour Vegetable Pancakes

Needs some time • Easy to make

• For the pancakes, stir eggs, flour, ½ teaspoon salt, and milk together until smooth. Add enough water to make a thin batter, cover, and let stand for about 30 minutes.

• Meanwhile, wash the vegetables and trim. Cut the kohlrabi into sticks, the scallions into pieces, and the bell pepper into strips. Wash the bean sprouts and drain the baby corn. Peel the garlic and ginger, and mince both fine.

• First heat the wok and then heat 2 tablespoons oil in it. Fry the garlic and ginger in the oil. Stir-fry the vegetables for 4 minutes. Add the soy sauce, vinegar, sugar, and broth, and let boil down briefly. Season with salt and pepper. Remove the vegetables from the wok and keep warm, covered. Clean the wok.

• Preheat the oven to 200°F (100°C). Heat the oil for the pancakes in the wok. In batches, over medium heat, form eight pancakes at a time from one ladleful of batter, sprinkling the batter with some sesame seeds just before turning. Keep the cooked pancakes warm, covered, on a platter in the warm oven. When all the pancakes are cooked, distribute the vegetables over the pancakes, roll them up, and sprinkle them with the rest of the sesame seeds.

Makes 4 servings.

For the pancakes:
4 small eggs
2 cups (9 oz/250 g) all-purpose flour
salt
1½ cups (12 fl oz/350 ml) milk
6–10 Tbs water
2 Tbs oil
2 Tbs sesame seeds

For the vegetables:
14 oz (400 g) kohlrabi
1 bunch scallions
1 red bell pepper
5 oz (150 g) fresh bean sprouts
8–10 baby corn ears (bottled)
1 garlic clove
1 piece fresh ginger (about 1 in/3 cm)
2 Tbs oil
¼ cup (60 ml) light soy sauce
4-5 Tbs white wine vinegar
1 heaping Tbs sugar
½ cup (4 oz/125 ml) vegetable broth
salt
pepper

Preparation time: about 50 minutes

PER SERVING:	566 CALORIES
NUTRITIONAL INFORMATION	

Fat (35% calories from fat) 23	g
Protein 25	g
Carbohydrate 71	g
Cholesterol 193	mg
Sodium 1173	mg

Vegetable Curry

1¾ lb (800 g) mixed
vegetables (according to
season)
1 onion
1–2 garlic cloves
1 Tbs oil
1⅔ cups (13½ fl oz/400 ml)
canned unsweetened coconut
milk
1 Tbs Thai green curry paste
½ tsp palm sugar or brown
sugar
salt
light soy sauce
pepper
1 bunch Thai basil or
cilantro

*Preparation time:
about 30 minutes*

Fried Artichokes

1 lb (450 g) firm-cooking
potatoes
1 tomato
6–7 small artichokes
4 Tbs olive oil
1 Tbs lemon juice
salt
pepper
1 Tbs chopped chives

*Preparation time:
about 35 minutes
(+ cooling time:
preferably overnight)*

Vegetable Curry

From Thailand • Hot

• Trim the vegetables and cut into bite-size pieces. Peel the onion and garlic and chop fine.

• First heat the wok and then heat the oil in it. Fry the onion and garlic in the oil. Stir in 1 cup (8 fl oz/250 mL) coconut milk and the curry paste and let simmer until the oil collects on top. Stir in the remaining coconut milk, the sugar, some salt, and the soy sauce. Add the vegetables and cook, stirring, over medium heat until they are softened but still firm to the bite.

• Season the vegetable curry to taste with salt and pepper. Pull the herb leaves from the stems and fold them in. Serve the curry with Thai fragrant rice.

Makes 4 servings.

Fried Artichokes

Subtle • Pictured

• Cook the potatoes, unpeeled, in a little water the day before.

• Peel the potatoes and dice. Scald the tomato, peel, remove the stem base and seeds, and dice. Remove the hard outer leaves from the artichokes and break off the stalks. Cut the artichokes lengthwise in very thin slices.

• First heat the wok and then heat 3 tablespoons oil in it. Stir-fry the artichokes until golden brown on both sides. Season with lemon juice, salt, and pepper. Remove the artichokes and keep warm.

• Heat the remaining tablespoon of oil in the wok. Fry the potatoes until crisp, turning constantly. Season well with salt and pepper. Briefly heat the artichokes in the wok with the potatoes. Sprinkle the whole dish with chives and tomato cubes.

Makes 4 servings.

PER SERVING:	393 CALORIES
NUTRITIONAL INFORMATION	
Fat (58% calories from fat) 27	g
Protein 10	g
Carbohydrate 36	g
Cholesterol 0	mg
Sodium 265	mg

PER SERVING:	219 CALORIES
NUTRITIONAL INFORMATION	
Fat (29% calories from fat) 8	g
Protein 7	g
Carbohydrate 35	g
Cholesterol 0	mg
Sodium 148	mg

Savoy Cabbage in Coconut Milk

Delicate • Pictured

• Trim the cabbage, quarter, wash, and cut into strips the width of a finger. Peel onions and garlic and chop. Trim the chili and cut into very fine strips.

• First heat the wok and then heat the oil in it. Stir-fry the cabbage for 5 minutes. Add the onions, garlic, and chili and stir-fry another 2 minutes.

• Pour in the coconut milk. Add the lemon peel and some salt. Cook over medium heat, stirring occasionally, until the cabbage is soft but still firm to the bite. Season with salt and pepper. Cut the coconut meat very thin with a mandoline. Sprinkle the shavings of coconut over the cabbage. Serve with Basmati rice.

Makes 4 servings.

Mushroom Fry

Fast • Easy to make

• Trim the mushrooms, wash briefly if necessary, and slice thin. Trim the celery, wash, and cut into sections about ¼ in (1 cm) wide, saving a few leaves; coarsely chop the leaves. Peel the onion and dice fine.

• First heat the wok and then heat the oil in it. Fry the onion until transparent. Add the mushrooms and stir-fry over higher heat until all liquid has evaporated.

• Mix in the celery. Add coriander and lemon juice. Stir-fry the mixture for about 2 minutes. Pour in the broth and cream and bring to a vigorous boil. Season the mushrooms to taste with salt and pepper and sprinkle with the reserved chopped celery leaves. Mashed potato tastes good with this, or a hearty bread.

Makes 4 servings.

Savoy Cabbage in Coconut Milk

*1 savoy cabbage
(about 1¾ lb/800 g)*
2 onions
1–2 garlic cloves
1 fresh red chili
3 Tbs oil
*1⅔ cups (13½ fl oz/400 ml)
canned unsweetened coconut
milk*
½ tsp grated lemon peel
salt
pepper
*2 oz (60 g) fresh coconut,
shredded or grated*

*Preparation time:
about 35 minutes*

Mushroom Fry

*18 oz (500 g) mixed
mushrooms (buttons, fresh
shiitakes, oyster mushrooms,
chanterelles)*
8 oz (250 g) celery
1 onion
2 Tbs oil
6 coriander seeds, crushed
1–2 Tbs lemon juice
3 Tbs vegetable broth
7 Tbs cream
salt
pepper

*Preparation time:
about 30 minutes*

PER SERVING:	369 CALORIES	
NUTRITIONAL INFORMATION		
Fat (72% calories from fat)	32	g
Protein	7	g
Carbohydrate	21	g
Cholesterol	0	mg
Sodium	337	mg

PER SERVING:	256 CALORIES	
NUTRITIONAL INFORMATION		
Fat (35% calories from fat)	11	g
Protein	7	g
Carbohydrate	39	g
Cholesterol	22	mg
Sodium	291	mg

Asparagus with Cloud Ear Mushrooms

½ oz (14 g) dried cloud ear mushrooms
1 lb 10 oz (750 g) green asparagus
2 garlic cloves
1 piece fresh ginger (size of a hazelnut)
4 Tbs oil
7 Tbs vegetable broth
1 Tbs light soy sauce
2 Tbs white wine vinegar
1 Tbs sesame oil
salt
pepper
2 Tbs chopped chives

*Preparation time:
about 40 minutes*

Couscous

salt
14 oz (400 g) quick couscous
¼ cup (2 oz/50 g) raisins
1 cup (8 fl oz/250 g) heavy cream or crème fraîche
cayenne pepper
2 red bell peppers
2 onions
2 small zucchini
½ bunch parsley
¼ cup (2 oz/50 g) shelled almonds
3 Tbs olive oil
6 Tbs vegetable broth
2–3 Tbs lemon juice
pepper

*Preparation time:
about 35 minutes*

Asparagus with Cloud Ear Mushrooms

For company • Pictured

• Pour boiling water over the dried mushrooms and let soften for about 30 minutes. Meanwhile, peel the lower third of the asparagus spears and cut diagonally into pieces about 1½ in (4 cm) long. Peel the garlic and mince.

• First heat the wok and then heat 2 tablespoons oil in it. Fry the garlic in the oil until golden brown; remove and set aside. Add the remaining oil to the wok and stir-fry the asparagus pieces for 5 minutes. Drain the mushrooms, rinse briefly, and pull apart into large pieces. Add to the wok with the ginger and fry all together briefly. Add the broth and cook the asparagus, covered, over medium heat, for 2 to 3 minutes until just barely soft.

• Mix the soy sauce, vinegar, and sesame oil and pour over the asparagus. Season to taste with salt and pepper. Sprinkle the garlic and chives over the top.

Makes 4 servings.

PER SERVING:	133 CALORIES
NUTRITIONAL INFORMATION	
Fat (58% calories from fat) 9	g
Protein 4	g
Carbohydrate 12	g
Cholesterol 0	mg
Sodium 385	mg

Couscous with Vegetables

North African • Subtle

• Bring 1¾ cups (14 fl oz/400 ml) lightly salted water to the boil. Pour it over the couscous and let soak, covered, until all the water is absorbed. Also soak the raisins to soften.

• Meanwhile, season the cream with cayenne pepper. Wash and trim the vegetables. Cut the peppers into strips and the onions into rings. Quarter the zucchini lengthwise and cut into pieces ½ in (2 cm) long. Pull off the parsley leaves; coarsely chop the almonds.

• Heat the wok and brown the almonds in it without oil until they are golden brown; remove and set aside. Heat the oil in the wok and stir-fry the vegetables in it for several minutes. Pour in the broth. Fluff the couscous, drain the raisins, and stir both into the wok. Heat for about 5 minutes, stirring constantly. Season with lemon juice, salt, and pepper, and fold in the almonds and parsley. Serve with the cream.

Makes 4 servings.

PER SERVING:	505 CALORIES
NUTRITIONAL INFORMATION	
Fat (50% calories from fat) 29	g
Protein 12	g
Carbohydrate 52	g
Cholesterol 50	mg
Sodium 186	mg

Ricotta Schmarren with Kiwi Puree

From Austria • Fast

• Peel the kiwis, dice, and puree. Season to taste with lemon juice and sugar. Chill the kiwi puree, covered.

• Separate 2 eggs. Beat 2 whole eggs with the 2 yolks until fluffy. Add the remaining sugar, salt, and lemon peel. Gradually stir in the milk, flour, almonds, and ricotta. Using clean beaters, beat the egg whites until stiff and gently fold into the dough.

• First heat the wok, and then melt the butter in it over medium heat. Pour in the batter and cook gently until the bottom is light yellow. Then quarter and pull into pieces with two forks. Fry the pieces of dough, turning constantly, until golden yellow and crisp. Dust with powdered sugar and serve with kiwi puree.

Makes 4 servings.

Variation

Instead of kiwi puree, serve a raspberry puree made with 9 to 10 oz (250 to 300 g) berries.

PER SERVING:	462 CALORIES	
NUTRITIONAL INFORMATION		
Fat (41% calories from fat)	22	g
Protein	17	g
Carbohydrate	52	g
Cholesterol	230	mg
Sodium	177	mg

Caramelized Fruit Salad

Fast • Pictured

• Peel and slice the banana. Wash the apple, quarter it, remove the core, and cut into slices without peeling. Wash the pear, peel, quarter, core, and dice. Peel the orange and kiwis; remove the membranes from the orange sections. Wash the grapes, halve, and seed if necessary. Peel the pineapple and cut the flesh into small pieces. Cut the herb leaves into fine strips.

• Heat the wok and caramelize the sugar over medium heat, stirring constantly, until it is golden yellow. Stirring vigorously, add the lemon juice.

• Warm the fruit and nuts in the caramel mixture, stirring constantly. Sprinkle with lemon balm. If desired, serve with lemon yogurt or vanilla ice cream.

Makes 4 servings.

Variation

Serve the salad in a hollowed-out pineapple half.

PER SERVING:	207 CALORIES	
NUTRITIONAL INFORMATION		
Fat (11% calories from fat)	3	g
Protein	2	g
Carbohydrate	48	g
Cholesterol	0	mg
Sodium	4	mg

COVERS on!

Braising

Braising is done in the wok when a lightning-quick stir-fry isn't long enough to get things cooked. The ingredients are fried briefly in little fat, seasoned, doused with liquid, and then further cooked over low heat. The highly conductive metal of the wok distributes the heat evenly to the ingredients. The cooking time can range from 3 to 30 minutes. Because even a half hour is still fast, the process is also referred to as quick-braising.

With a Cover or Without?

If the dish is braised without a cover, the liquid reduces, and the resulting sauce is thickened and flavorful. If cooking is done with a cover, it is crucial to success that the cover be tightly closed. The best cover is a curved one, so that condensation runs down its sides and doesn't drop from the top into the dish. With cooking times of more than 5 minutes, stir a few times during the braising so that nothing sticks.

Suitable Vegetables

Firm vegetables such as carrots, celery, onions, leeks, fennel, brussels sprouts, red cabbage, and kale are good for quick braising. In this process, spices also have enough time to release their flavor completely and penetrate the vegetables.

Small Portions

Vegetables must be dry for frying (if necessary, pat dry with paper towels after cutting) so that the fat doesn't spatter in the wok. Vegetables are best fried in several batches, separated according to variety. If you put everything in the wok at once, the fat cools, the vegetable juices leak out, and the ingredients simmer rather than fry.

Be Sparing with Salt and Pepper

Only season a braised dish with salt and pepper at the end. If you season strongly at first, the taste can become too intense as the liquid evaporates.

Braising Liquids

Water serves well as a braising liquid, but more flavorful are vegetable broth (basic recipe at the right), vegetable juices, yogurt, red or white wine or cider, or a mixture of broth and wine. The alcohol evaporates during the cooking, but the flavor remains.

Asian Seasonings

A few recipes in this chapter are prepared with typical Asian seasonings.

• Chilis are always fiery hot, fresh as well as dried. The smaller the peppers, the hotter they are. The equally hot cayenne pepper is produced from ground chilis.

• Ginger is a root tuber with a robust flavor and slight heat. It is fresh when it has a taut, smooth skin.

• Curry powder is a spice mixture of up to 36 different ingredients, which in India is prepared fresh for every dish. We usually buy it ready-made. Depending on the constituents, the mixture may be mild or hot.

• Curry paste is available in Asian stores in differing compositions. It keeps in the refrigerator for several months.

• Cumin is an ingredient in almost all curry mixtures that goes especially well with vegetables.

• Turmeric, a yellow-orange root, is available in the West only in powdered form.

• Cilantro, sometimes sold as coriander greens or Chinese parsley, is an aromatic herb with an unmistakable flavor. You can find it in supermarkets or in Asian or Latino groceries.

Vegetable Broth—Basic Recipe

Ingredients for 2–3 cups
(16–24 fl oz/500–750 ml):
2 carrots
2 leeks
1 onion
4-6 fresh button mushrooms
½ celery root
2 Tbs butter
1 bay leaf
4 black peppercorns
1 tsp light soy sauce
6 cups (48 fl oz/1.5 l) water
5–6 parsley stalks

Clean the vegetables, wash briefly, and cut into small pieces. Melt the butter in a soup kettle and gently fry the carrots, leeks, onion, and mushrooms until light brown. Add all the remaining ingredients, bring to a boil, and simmer, covered, for 1 hour. Strain the broth into a second pot and boil uncovered until reduced by half. Do not salt the vegetable broth. You can vary it according to season and what is available. Store the broth in the refrigerator in a tightly closed container for up to 3 days, or freeze it.

Red Cabbage with Gorgonzola

1 small red cabbage
(about 1¾ lb/800 g)
3 oranges
2 Tbs vinegar
salt
pepper
1 bunch scallions
2 Tbs clarified butter
5 Tbs cream
7 oz (200 g) Gorgonzola or
other blue cheese, crumbled

*Preparation time:
about 55 minutes*

Braised Swiss Chard

1¾ lb (800 g) Swiss chard
1 lb (450 g) firm-cooking
potatoes
1 onion
2 garlic cloves
5 Tbs olive oil
¼ cup (2 oz/50 g) whole
blanched almonds
salt
1⅔ cups (13 fl oz/400 ml)
vegetable broth
lemon juice
pepper

*Preparation time:
about 45 minutes*

Red Cabbage with Gorgonzola

Unusual • Pictured

• Clean the red cabbage, quarter it, and shave very fine with a vegetable grater or mandoline. Squeeze 2 oranges and mix the juice into the red cabbage along with the vinegar, salt, and pepper. Marinate, covered, for about 20 minutes.

• Meanwhile, peel the scallions, wash, and cut them into thin rings. Peel the third orange, section it, and cut the sections in half crosswise. Drain the red cabbage in a sieve, catching and reserving the liquid.

• First heat the wok and then heat the clarified butter in it. Stir-fry the cabbage in batches over medium heat. Add the onions and the reserved liquid, cover, and braise 5 to 7 minutes. Fold in the cream and the orange sections. Season the cabbage to taste with salt and pepper. Sprinkle the cheese over it in small pieces and allow to melt, covered. Serve with sunflower-seed or other whole-grain bread.

Makes 4 servings.

PER SERVING:	376 CALORIES	
NUTRITIONAL INFORMATION		
Fat (64% calories from fat) 28		g
Protein 13		g
Carbohydrate 22		g
Cholesterol 34		mg
Sodium 29		mg

Braised Swiss Chard

From Spain • Easy to make

• Trim the chard and wash. Remove the stems from the leaves and cut the stems into strips ¼ in (1 cm) wide. Cut the leaves into broad strips. Peel the potatoes and dice them fine. Peel and chop the onion and garlic.

• First heat the wok, then heat 2 tablespoons oil in it. Briefly brown the almonds; remove and set aside. Fry the chard stems and potatoes in the oil, stirring, for 3 minutes. Add the onion and garlic and fry briefly together.

• Distribute the chard leaves over the vegetables with the almonds, and salt lightly. Add the broth and braise the vegetables, covered, over moderate heat for about 15 minutes or until the potatoes are soft.

• Take the chard from the stove. Stir in lemon juice to taste with salt, pepper, and the remaining oil.

Makes 4 servings.

PER SERVING:	194 CALORIES	
NUTRITIONAL INFORMATION		
Fat (49% calories from fat) 11		g
Protein 6		g
Carbohydrate 20		g
Cholesterol 1		mg
Sodium 1228		mg

Caramel Potatoes

Pictured • Easy to make

• Cook the potatoes in their skins in a little water for about 20 minutes.

• Wash the carrots and celery, trim, and cut into pencil-thick pieces about 1½ in (4 cm) long. First heat the wok, then heat 1 tablespoon butter in it. Stir-fry the vegetables briefly without browning. Add pepper and the broth and cook the vegetables over low heat, covered, for about 7 minutes; they should still be crisp. Season with salt, remove from the wok, and keep warm.

• Peel the potatoes. Let the sugar melt in the wok until it is golden yellow. Add the remaining butter and deglaze with wine. Add the potatoes to the caramel and braise, covered, for about 5 minutes, turning now and then.

• Add the vegetables to the potatoes in the wok and heat briefly. Pepper all lightly and sprinkle with the sunflower seeds.

Makes 4 servings.

Kale with Tomatoes

Inexpensive • Hearty

• Bring salted water to the boil.

• Remove stems and thick ribs from the kale. Wash the leaves very thoroughly, then blanch in salted water for 5 minutes. Drain and press out all moisture, then chop coarsely. Peel the onion, garlic, and carrot and dice fine. Clean and finely chop the leek and parsley.

• First heat the wok and then heat the butter in it. Stir-fry the onion, garlic, and carrot for about 2 minutes without browning. Add the kale, tomatoes, leek, parsley, broth, and thyme. Season lightly with salt and pepper. Braise, covered, over moderate heat for about 15 minutes.

• Uncover and let the kale cook down until creamy. Season to taste with sugar, salt, and pepper. Serve with mashed potatoes.

Makes 4 servings.

Caramel Potatoes

1½ lb (700 g) small, firm-cooking potatoes
3 carrots
3 stalks celery
3 Tbs butter
pepper
7 Tbs vegetable broth
salt
¼ cup (2 oz/60 g) sugar
2 Tbs white wine or water
2 Tbs coarsely chopped sunflower seeds

*Preparation time:
about 30 minutes*

Kale with Tomatoes

salt
1¾ lb (800 g) kale
1 onion
1 garlic clove
1 small carrot
1 leek
several sprigs parsley
2 Tbs butter
1 can (14 oz/400 g) peeled tomatoes, drained
1 cup (250 ml) vegetable broth
1 tsp chopped fresh thyme
pepper
½ tsp sugar

*Preparation time:
about 1 hour*

PER SERVING:	300 CALORIES	
NUTRITIONAL INFORMATION		
Fat (35% calories from fat) 12	g
Protein 5	g
Carbohydrate 45	g
Cholesterol 28	mg
Sodium 326	mg

PER SERVING:	189 CALORIES	
NUTRITIONAL INFORMATION		
Fat (34% calories from fat) 8	g
Protein 7	g
Carbohydrate 27	g
Cholesterol 16	mg
Sodium 851	mg

Chili con Tofu

Chili con Tofu
7 oz (200 g) dried kidney beans
9 oz (250 g) tofu
3 onions
2–3 garlic cloves
2–3 chilis or small hot red peppers
1 each yellow and green bell pepper
2 Tbs oil
1 can (14 oz/400 g) peeled tomatoes
1¾–2 cups (14–16 fl oz/ 400–500 ml) vegetable broth
salt
pepper

Preparation time:
about 1 hour and 20 minutes (+ overnight soaking time)

Leeks Siciliana

Leeks Siciliana
3 Tbs golden raisins
2 lb (1 kg) thin leeks
1–2 garlic cloves
2 Tbs pine nuts
3 Tbs olive oil
salt
pepper
2 tsp grated lemon peel
2–3 Tbs lemon juice
½ bunch parsley, chopped fine

Preparation time:
about 35 minutes

Chili con Tofu
A new version of a classic • Pictured

• Wash the beans and soak overnight in 1 quart (1 liter) water. The next day simmer 1 hour, covered, in the soaking water.

• Meanwhile, dice the tofu. Peel the onions and garlic; cut onions into eighths. Remove the seeds from the chilis and mince fine with the garlic. Wash the peppers, quarter, seed, and cut into strips.

• First heat the wok and then heat the oil in it. Fry the tofu briefly in the oil, then remove. Fry the chili-garlic mixture together until fragrant. Add the peppers and fry briefly. Add the drained cooked beans, the tomatoes with juice, and the vegetable broth. Season with salt and pepper and braise, covered, over medium heat for about 15 minutes. Stir in the tofu and season the chili to taste. Serve with corn tortillas or fluffy long-grain rice.

Makes 4 servings.

Leeks Siciliana
From Southern Italy • Refreshing

• Soften the raisins in water to cover. Meanwhile, trim the leeks, wash thoroughly, and cut on the diagonal into pieces about 1½ in (4 cm) long. Peel the garlic cloves.

• Heat the wok and roast the pine nuts in it without any oil until they are light yellow. Remove and set aside. Heat the oil in the wok and stir-fry the leeks without letting them brown. Season with salt and pepper. Put the garlic through a garlic press into the wok.

• Drain the raisins and add to the vegetables with the lemon peel. Cover and braise until the leeks are crisp-tender. Season to taste with lemon juice and sprinkle with pine nuts and parsley. Serve with rice, potatoes, or pita bread.

Makes 4 servings.

PER SERVING:	307 CALORIES
NUTRITIONAL INFORMATION	
Fat (29% calories from fat) . . . . 10 g	
Protein . . . . 15 g	
Carbohydrate . . . . 41 g	
Cholesterol . . . . 1 mg	
Sodium . . . . 1060 mg	

PER SERVING:	175 CALORIES
NUTRITIONAL INFORMATION	
Fat (37% calories from fat) . . . . 8 g	
Protein . . . . 4 g	
Carbohydrate . . . . 26 g	
Cholesterol . . . . 0 mg	
Sodium . . . . 59 mg	

Cauliflower Curry

1 cauliflower
(about 2 lb/1 kg)
2 onions
1 fresh red chili
2 tomatoes
2 Tbs clarified butter
1 tsp freshly grated ginger
1 Tbs curry powder
½ tsp sugar
⅔ cup (5 fl oz/150 ml)
vegetable broth
5 oz (150 g) peas
salt
1 Tbs parsley leaves

Preparation time:
about 35 minutes

Eggplant

2 medium-sized eggplants
1½ tsp salt
1 tsp yellow mustard seeds
1 tsp cumin seeds
4–5 Tbs oil
4 Tbs mustard oil (or
substitute 2 Tbs clarified
butter)
1 tsp freshly grated ginger
3 dried red chilis, crumbled
1 tsp paprika
½ tsp turmeric
¼ tsp cayenne pepper
⅔ cup (5 oz/150 g) whole-
milk yogurt
2 Tbs cilantro leaves

Preparation time:
about 40 minutes

Cauliflower Curry

From India • Hot

• Cut the cauliflower into little rosettes, wash, and drain. Peel the onions and seed the chili. Cut both into fine strips. Scald the tomatoes, peel, and dice, removing seeds and stem bases.

• First heat the wok and then heat the clarified butter in it. Stir-fry the onions, chili, and ginger in it briefly. Stir in the curry powder and sugar and cook over low heat for 2 minutes.

• Fold the cauliflower into the mixture and add the tomatoes and broth. Braise all over medium heat, stirring occasionally, for about 10 minutes.

• Add the peas to the curry and braise only until the cauliflower is cooked but still firm to the bite. Season to taste with salt and sprinkle with parsley. Serve with Basmati rice.

Makes 4 servings.

PER SERVING:	210 CALORIES	
NUTRITIONAL INFORMATION		
Fat (33% calories from fat) 9		g
Protein 9		g
Carbohydrate 29		g
Cholesterol 18		mg
Sodium 613		mg

Eggplant in Mustard-Yogurt Sauce

From India • Pictured

• Peel the eggplant and cut lengthwise into strips about ¼ in (1 cm) thick. Sprinkle with salt and let stand for about 10 minutes. Meanwhile roast the mustard seeds and cumin seeds in the dry wok until they begin to jump. Remove and let cool.

• Carefully press the liquid out of the eggplant and pat it dry. Heat the oil in the wok and fry the eggplant in it over high heat on both sides until golden brown. Drain on paper towels. Pour off any leftover oil.

• Heat the mustard oil in the wok and fry the ginger and chilis in it. Lightly brown the remaining spices with them, stirring. Deglaze with yogurt and ½ cup (4 fl oz/125 ml) water. Bring to a boil and simmer for 5 minutes.

• Grind mustard and cumin seeds fine and stir in. Cover and let eggplant braise in the sauce over low heat for another 5 minutes. Sprinkle with cilantro and serve.

Makes 4 servings.

PER SERVING:	236 CALORIES	
NUTRITIONAL INFORMATION		
Fat (65% calories from fat) 18		g
Protein 4		g
Carbohydrate 18		g
Cholesterol 22		mg
Sodium 28		mg

Squash Ratatouille

2 meaty tomatoes
2 onions
2 garlic cloves
1 green bell pepper
1¼ lb (600 g) peeled and seeded acorn or butternut squash
½ bunch parsley
3 Tbs olive oil
salt
pepper
1 bay leaf
1 sprig thyme

Preparation time:
about 45 minutes

Vegetable Risotto

1 Tbs dried mixed mushrooms
1 onion
1 garlic clove
5 oz (150 g) each celery root and carrots
3 Tbs butter
1 generous cup (9 oz/250 g) seven-grain cereal, uncooked
1⅔ cups (13 fl oz/400 ml) vegetable broth
2 tomatoes
2 oz (60 g) Emmentaler cheese, freshly grated
1 Tbs crème fraîche
salt
pepper

Preparation time:
about 45 minutes

Squash Ratatouille

A new version of a classic • Pictured

• Scald the tomatoes, peel, and dice, removing seeds and stem bases. Peel the onions and garlic; cut onions into eighths. Quarter the peppers, wash, seed, and cut into strips. Cut the squash into 1-in (3-cm) cubes. Strip off the parsley leaves, reserving the stems.

• First heat the wok and then heat the oil in it. Briefly stir-fry the vegetables in batches. Add salt and pepper, put the garlic through the press into the wok, and add 7 tablespoons water. Tie the bay leaf, thyme, and parsley stems into a bouquet and lay it in the wok. Braise the vegetables, covered, over low heat for about 25 minutes.

• Season the ratatouille with salt and pepper to taste and fold in the parsley leaves. Serve with rice or French bread.

Makes 4 servings.

PER SERVING:	134 CALORIES
NUTRITIONAL INFORMATION	
Fat (38% calories from fat) 6	g
Protein 4	g
Carbohydrate 19	g
Cholesterol 0	mg
Sodium 317	mg

Vegetable Risotto with Grain

Easy to make • Needs some time

• Pour boiling water over the dried mushrooms and let them soften. Meanwhile, peel the onion and garlic and mince. Wash the celery root and carrots, peel, and cut into small cubes.

• First heat the wok and then heat 2 tablespoons butter in it. Fry the onion and garlic until transparent. Add the celery root and carrots and stir-fry 2 minutes. Stir in the cereal mixture and the drained mushrooms. Pour in the broth and bring to a boil. Cook, covered, over low heat for 20 to 25 minutes or until the broth is absorbed.

• Meanwhile, wash and dice the tomatoes. Fold them into the risotto along with the remaining butter, cheese, and the crème fraîche; season with salt and pepper.

Makes 4 servings.

PER SERVING:	520 CALORIES
NUTRITIONAL INFORMATION	
Fat (30% calories from fat) 18	g
Protein 20	g
Carbohydrate 75	g
Cholesterol 40	mg
Sodium 1005	mg

Brussels Sprouts Curry

Sophisticated · Hot

• Wash and seed the chilis; cut into fine rings. Peel the ginger, garlic, and shallots and chop fine. Peel the potatoes and carrots and cut into small cubes. Trim and wash the brussels sprouts; halve the larger ones.

• First heat the wok and then heat the clarified butter in it. Stir-fry the chilis, ginger, garlic, and shallots until fragrant. Stir in curry and turmeric. Deglaze the wok with the broth and milk. Add the potatoes and carrots, bring to a boil, and simmer, covered, over moderate heat for 10 minutes.

• Add the brussels sprouts to the wok and cook until tender but still firm to the bite, 10 to 15 minutes longer. Fold the crème fraîche and chives gently into the vegetables.

Makes 4 servings.

Fennel with Honey

Easy to make · Pictured

• Bring a large pot of salted water to a boil.

• Trim and wash the fennel bulb. Halve it and cut out the stalk base. Set the greens aside. Drop the bulb halves into the boiling water and cook 5 minutes. Drain the fennel, reserving ½ cup (4 fl oz/125 ml) of the cooking water.

• Heat the wok. Roast the pine nuts in it without oil until golden; remove and set them aside. Heat the oil in the wok. Fry the fennel over moderate heat, turning constantly. Stir in the fennel seeds and briefly cook together. Add the cooking water and honey. Season with salt and pepper. Cook the fennel, covered, for 5 to 7 minutes or until crisp-tender.

• Wash the fennel greens and tear them into large pieces. Scatter them over the fennel along with the pine nuts.

Makes 4 servings.

Brussels Sprouts Curry

2 fresh red chilis
1 piece fresh ginger (about 1 in/3 cm long)
1–2 garlic cloves
2 shallots
1 lb (450 g) potatoes
3 large carrots
1 lb 10 oz (750 g) brussels sprouts
1 Tbs clarified butter
1 tsp each hot curry powder and turmeric
2 cups (16 fl oz/500 ml) vegetable broth
1⅔ cups (13 fl oz/400 ml) milk
2–3 Tbs crème fraîche or sour cream
1 Tbs chopped chives

Preparation time: about 50 minutes

Fennel with Honey

salt
2 lb (900 g) small fennel bulbs
1½ oz (40 g) pine nuts
3 Tbs oil
2 tsp fennel seeds
1 Tbs honey
pepper

Preparation time: about 40 minutes

PER SERVING:	372 CALORIES
NUTRITIONAL INFORMATION	

Fat (28% calories from fat)	12	g
Protein	15	g
Carbohydrate	56	g
Cholesterol	33	mg
Sodium	812	mg

PER SERVING:	140 CALORIES
NUTRITIONAL INFORMATION	

Fat (55% calories from fat)	9	g
Protein	3	g
Carbohydrate	15	g
Cholesterol	0	mg
Sodium	89	mg

Apple Ragout

1 egg
2 cups (16 fl oz/500 mL) milk
5 Tbs sugar
pinch of salt
1 piece lemon peel
1 tsp vanilla extract
¼ cup (1½ oz/45 g) semolina,
farina, or Cream of Wheat
1¾ lb (800 g) flavorful apples
2–3 Tbs lemon juice
2 Tbs butter
½ cup (4 fl oz/125 ml) dry
white wine or water
⅔ cup (5 oz/150 g) cream
2 Tbs grated hazelnuts

Preparation time:
about 35 minutes

Sweet Risotto

1 Tbs butter
1½ cups (10 oz/300 g) risotto
rice
1 cup (8 fl oz/250 ml) milk
pinch of salt
1 vanilla bean
7 oz (200 g) ripe apricots
1 generous pound (500 g)
strawberries
2–3 Tbs powdered sugar
1–2 Tbs lemon juice
2 Tbs crème fraîche or
sour cream
2 Tbs chopped pistachio nuts

Preparation time:
about 30 minutes

Apple Ragout on Vanilla Semolina Pudding

For children • Inexpensive

• For the pudding, separate the egg. Beat the yolk with a little of the milk. Bring the remaining milk, 2 tablespoons sugar, salt, and lemon peel to boil in a saucepan. Add the semolina and cook over low heat, stirring, for about 3 minutes. Remove from heat and stir in the beaten yolk mixture and vanilla. Beat the egg white stiff and fold in.

• For the apple ragout, peel, core, and quarter the apples. Slice about ¼ in (1 cm) thick. Mix with lemon juice to keep apples from discoloring.

• Heat the wok and let the butter foam over medium heat. Fry the apples briefly, turning constantly, without browning. Add the remaining sugar, wine, and cream, and braise the apples, covered, for 2 minutes or until soft but not mushy. Sprinkle with grated hazelnuts. Serve the apple ragout on the warm pudding.

Makes 4 servings.

PER SERVING:	623 CALORIES	
NUTRITIONAL INFORMATION		
Fat (47% calories from fat) 26		g
Protein. 8		g
Carbohydrate 59		g
Cholesterol 213		mg
Sodium 1		mg

Sweet Risotto with Strawberry Puree

Easy to make • Pictured

• First heat the wok and then heat the butter in it. Stir-fry the rice for 2 minutes or until transparent.

• Mix the milk with 1 cup (8 fl oz/250 ml) water and the salt and add to the rice. Slit open the vanilla bean lengthwise and add. Cover and cook, over moderate heat, stirring every now and then, until the rice grains are soft on the outside but still firm to the bite inside, 15 to 20 minutes.

• Meanwhile, scald the apricots and remove the skins. Halve the apricots and remove the stones, then cut the fruit into sections. Wash, hull, and quarter the strawberries. Puree half the strawberries with powdered sugar and lemon juice.

• Fold the apricot sections, quartered strawberries, and crème fraîche into the risotto and heat briefly. Scatter the chopped pistachios over the risotto and serve with the strawberry puree.

Makes 4 servings.

PER SERVING:	454 CALORIES	
NUTRITIONAL INFORMATION		
Fat (19% calories from fat) 10		g
Protein. 9		g
Carbohydrate 82		g
Cholesterol 26		mg
Sodium 79		mg

Tender Beneath a Crunchy
CRUST

Deep-Frying

Deep-frying is just as popular in the homeland of the wok as it is in the American kitchen. In deep-frying, oil is heated and the ingredients are cooked in it, floating, until they turn golden. Most deep-frying is done at temperatures of 340° to 356°F (170° to 180°C), but for delicate fruits 320° to 340°F (160° to 170°C) is enough. The heat shock causes the outer surface to seal immediately. It develops a crunchy protective crust, which does not allow the fat to penetrate, and inside everything remains crisp and juicy.

The Wok's Advantages
The wok is especially well suited for deep-frying, with decided advantages over pots and frying pans: Because of the taper at the bottom, less oil is necessary—depending on the diameter of the wok, only up to about 2 cups (16 fl oz/500 ml). At the same time there is a large "swimming surface" for the ingredients. Besides, the wok is wide and high enough so that nothing can boil over.

Useful Utensils
For deep-frying you need a shallow skimmer to put the food into the fat, swish it back and forth, and take it out again when cooked.

Also useful is a fat thermometer with markings up to 572°F (300°C), in order to be able to read the exact temperature. Fat thermometers are available at well-stocked housewares stores. If you have no thermometer, use a wooden spoon. When you hold the spoon in the fat and no small bubbles climb up it, the fat is about 356°F (180°C).

A semicircular drip screen is practical, but this usually comes with the wok.

Use the Right Oil
A high-quality oil is crucial to good results; it must be taste-neutral and able to be heated to above 392°F (200°C). Butter or margarine is unsuitable; they burn and break down at 212°F (100°C). Use fresh vegetable oil or clarified butter. Under no

circumstances should you mix different kinds of fat or mix used with fresh—because of their different boiling points, the mixture can spatter and boil over.

Coatings of Dough, Breading, or . . .

Ingredients that are rich in protein (eggs) or starch (potatoes, beets) can be fried without any coatings. All others are more successful with a protective covering: Either the item to be fried is drawn through a deep-frying batter or it is coated in a breading mixture. In this process it is important that the ingredients are all patted very dry and that the breading is firmly pressed on or the batter completely encloses the vegetable (but with the excess well drained). There is another variation in which the vegetable or fruit is wrapped in dough and fried as rolls or packets.

Frying Rules

• Heat the oil in a clean, dry wok to 356°F (180°C). It must never become smoking hot or overheated, since then there is the danger of fire.

• Always fry in small batches so that the oil won't cool off too much. The vegetables should bubble freely and quickly rise to the surface.

• If the vegetables sink to the bottom, the oil isn't hot enough. If they immediately turn brown, the temperature is too high.

• Move and turn the ingredients during frying so that they brown evenly. As you work, keep an eye on the temperature and regulate it as necessary.

• Lift the fried foods out with the skimmer and lay them to drain on the drip screen, in a sieve, or on several layers of paper towels.

• Put the already finished pieces in an ovenproof dish and keep them warm in the oven at 225°F (100°C).

• Remove any floating leftovers of batter or breading by continually swishing the skimmer through the hot oil.

Handling Used Oil

Strain the oil immediately after frying so that it can be used one or two more times. Pour cooled oil through a sieve lined with a coffee filter or a layer of paper towels. Put it in a jar or bottle, close it tightly, label it (date and how many times used) and store it in a cool, dark place. It will keep for about six months. The strained oil can also be used for shallow frying.

Used oil that is dark and that smokes or foams at 338°F (170°C) must be discarded. But please don't pour it down the drain. Put it into the garbage in a tightly closed container.

45

Oyster Mushrooms Piccata

1 lb 2 oz (500 g) oyster mushrooms

1 Tbs dried cepes or other dried mushrooms

4 eggs

2–4 Tbs milk

2 oz (60 g) freshly grated Parmesan or Gruyère cheese

pepper

1 tsp chopped fresh thyme

10 oz (300 g) cucumbers

1¼ cups (10 oz/300 g) whole-milk yogurt

salt

3 sprigs basil

1 lime or lemon

1 cup (8 oz/250 g) clarified butter

Preparation time: about 25 minutes

Crisp Black Salsify

3 Tbs white wine vinegar

2 lb (1 kg) black salsify

salt

1 small onion

2 Tbs oil

1 can (14 oz/400 g) peeled tomatoes

pinch of sugar

pepper

2 eggs

3 oz (85 g) pumpkin seeds

2–3 cups (16–24 fl oz/ 500–750 ml) oil for deep-frying

1 Tbs finely chopped parsley

Preparation time: about 45 minutes

Oyster Mushrooms Piccata

From Italy • Fast

• Carefully clean the mushrooms with paper towels or a brush and trim the end of the stems. Grind the cepes in a mortar or blender as fine as possible. Mix the eggs, milk, cheese, ½ teaspoon pepper, thyme, and mushroom powder.

• For the dip, peel, halve, and seed the cucumbers; dice fine. Stir with the yogurt and add salt and pepper. Wash the basil, chop the leaves coarsely, and stir them in. Wash the lime in hot water and slice it.

• First heat the wok and then heat the clarified butter in it. Dip the mushroom caps into the egg mixture in batches and deep-fry them on both sides until golden brown, about 3 minutes. Serve with the lime slices and cucumber dip. A salad and hearty whole-wheat bread go well with this.

Makes 4 servings.

PER SERVING:	395 CALORIES
NUTRITIONAL INFORMATION	
Fat (66% calories from fat) 28	g
Protein 18	g
Carbohydrate 15	g
Cholesterol 372	mg
Sodium 8	mg

Crisp Black Salsify

Pictured • Different

• Stir 1 quart (1 liter) water with the vinegar. Peel the salsify, wash, and immediately drop into the vinegar water. Cut into pieces 2 in (6 cm) long. Bring to a boil in the vinegar water in a pot or wok, add salt, and, depending on thickness, cook 12 to 15 minutes or until tender but not mushy. Drain.

• Peel the onion and chop fine. Heat the oil in a skillet and fry the onion until translucent. Add the tomatoes with juice, pressing with a fork to mash slightly. Stir in sugar, salt, and pepper. Simmer all together until creamy, stirring occasionally.

• Beat the eggs. Chop the pumpkin seeds. Roll the salsify in the eggs, then in the pumpkin seeds. First heat the wok and then heat the oil in it. Deep-fry the salsify in batches for 3 to 4 minutes, until golden. Drain. Stir parsley into the sauce and serve with the salsify.

Makes 4 servings.

PER SERVING:	319 CALORIES
NUTRITIONAL INFORMATION	
Fat (69% calories from fat) 25	g
Protein 12	g
Carbohydrate 14	g
Cholesterol 158	mg
Sodium 13	mg

Beets

5 oz (150 g) baking potatoes
1¼ lb (800 g) beets
2 egg yolks
1 Tbs white wine
pinch of sugar
salt
1 cup (5 oz/140 g) flour
1 tsp baking powder
3–4 Tbs (1½–2 fl oz/45–60 ml) milk
3 Tbs (1½ fl oz/50 ml) cream
1 Tbs small capers
1 tsp bottled horseradish
pepper
2 cups (16 fl oz/500 ml) oil for deep frying

Preparation time: about 1 hour

Skewered Vegetables

1 cup (5 oz/140 g) all purpose flour
½ cup (4 fl oz/125 ml) milk
2 Tbs melted butter
2 egg yolks
½ tsp coriander seeds
2 Tbs sesame seeds
soy sauce
pepper
10 oz (300 g) broccoli
7 oz (200 g) zucchini
2 carrots
8 button mushrooms
2 egg whites
1½–2 cups (12–16 fl oz/ 375–500 ml) oil for deep frying
wooden skewers/sticks

Preparation time: about 40 minutes

Beets with Whipped Potatoes

Elegant • For company

• Steam the potatoes and beets in the wok for 35 to 45 minutes; they should still be firm when poked.

• Mix the egg yolks, wine, sugar, 2 pinches salt, and ⅔ cup (5 fl oz/150 ml) very cold water until smooth. Sift in the flour and baking powder and stir to form a smooth batter, adding a little more water if batter is too thick. Peel and slice the beets.

• Peel the potatoes and put through a potato ricer into a wide pan, or mash. Heat the milk and add it with the cream to the potatoes, beating until smooth and creamy. Stir in the capers and horseradish. Season to taste with salt and pepper.

• First heat the wok and then heat the oil in it. Coat the beet slices in the batter and fry in the hot oil until golden, about 3 minutes, turning once. Drain on paper towels. Serve with the whipped potatoes.

Makes 4 servings.

PER SERVING:	380 CALORIES	
NUTRITIONAL INFORMATION		
Fat (36% calories from fat) 15		g
Protein 10		g
Carbohydrate 49		g
Cholesterol 172		mg
Sodium 20		mg

Skewered Vegetables in Sesame Batter

Pictured • Inexpensive

• Mix the flour, milk, melted butter, egg yolks, and about 7 tablespoons water to form a smooth batter. Crush the coriander seeds and stir into the batter with the sesame seeds; season with soy sauce.

• Wash the vegetables and trim. Cut the broccoli into small rosettes and the zucchini and carrots into slices. Halve any large mushrooms. Thread the vegetables, colorfully mixed, on wooden skewers that are not too long. Sprinkle with pepper.

• Beat the egg whites stiff and fold into the batter. First heat the wok, then heat the oil in it. Coat the skewered vegetables with the batter and fry them in batches, turning for about 6 minutes or until golden brown. Drain on paper towels and serve hot. A wild rice mixture and herb dip go well with them.

Makes 4 servings.

PER SERVING:	383 CALORIES	
NUTRITIONAL INFORMATION		
Fat (52% calories from fat) 21		g
Protein 13		g
Carbohydrate 31		g
Cholesterol 173		mg
Sodium 4		mg

Stuffed Zucchini Flowers

Something special • Pictured

• Coarsely chop the pistachios. Wash the basil and cut the leaves into fine strips. Wash the lemon under hot water, grate the peel, and squeeze the juice. Mix the cheese with 2 tablespoons lemon juice, the lemon peel, vinegar, pistachios, and basil until creamy, adding a little water if necessary. Season with salt and pepper.

• Clean the zucchini flowers, gently opening them and carefully removing the pistils. If necessary, cut away any fruit formation. Fill the flowers with the cheese mixture, then close the flowers again by twisting the tips of the petals together.

• First heat the wok, then heat the oil in it. Deep-fry the zucchini flowers in batches for about 1 minute. Drain on paper towels. Drizzle the rest of the lemon juice over them. Serve with mixed salad or arugula salad.

Makes 4 servings.

Deep-fried Vegetable Wontons

From China • Easy to make

• Let the wonton wrappers thaw, covered. Meanwhile, trim the Chinese cabbage and leeks and wash. Chop the cabbage very fine. Cut the leek into fine rings. Peel the carrot and mince fine. Mash the tofu. Separate the egg.

• Mix the cabbage, leek, carrot, chili, tofu, cornstarch, egg yolk, soy sauce, and sesame oil. Season with salt and pepper.

• Put 1 tablespoonful filling on each wonton wrapper, paint the edges with beaten egg white, and fold over each wonton, making a triangle.

• First heat the wok and then heat the oil in it. Deep-fry the wontons in batches for 2 to 3 minutes or until golden and crisp. A sweet-and-sour sauce and raw vegetables for nibbling go very well with this.

Makes 4 servings.

Stuffed Zucchini Flowers

2 Tbs pistachio nuts
1 sprig basil
1 lemon
7 oz (200 g) cream cheese or mascarpone
1 Tbs balsamic vinegar
salt
pepper
12 zucchini blossoms
1½–2 cups (12–16 fl oz/ 375–500 ml) oil for deep frying

Preparation time: about 25 minutes

Vegetable Wontons

20 frozen wonton wrappers (about 4 × 4 in/10 × 10 cm)
3 oz (90 g) Chinese (Napa) cabbage
3 oz (90 g) leek
1 carrot
4 oz (120 g) soft tofu (use smoked tofu if available)
1 egg
½ dried chili pepper, crumbled
1 tsp cornstarch
1 Tbs light soy sauce
1 tsp sesame oil
salt
pepper
oil for deep frying

Preparation time: about 30 minutes

PER SERVING:	277 CALORIES	
NUTRITIONAL INFORMATION		
Fat (86% calories from fat) 28	g
Protein 5	g
Carbohydrate 6	g
Cholesterol 55	mg
Sodium 149	mg

PER SERVING:	274 CALORIES	
NUTRITIONAL INFORMATION		
Fat (34% calories from fat) 10	g
Protein 12	g
Carbohydrate 33	g
Cholesterol 157	mg
Sodium 545	mg

51

For the batter:
3 Tbs butter
1¼ tsp dry yeast
½ tsp sugar
¾ cup (6 fl oz/180 ml)
lukewarm milk
¾ cup (3 oz/90 g) buckwheat
flour
1 cup (5 oz/140 g)
all-purpose flour
salt
2 egg whites

For the vegetables:
1 small head Chinese (Napa)
cabbage
1 onion
1 garlic clove
1 small red chili pepper
2 Tbs oil
3 Tbs vegetable broth
1–2 Tbs cream
salt
pepper
7 oz (200 g) clarified butter
for frying

Preparation time:
about 1¼ hours
(of which 1¼ hours is
resting time)

Little Yeast Cakes with Chinese Cabbage

Economical • Needs some time

• For the batter, melt the butter and let cool slightly. Dissolve the yeast and sugar in the milk. Blend the yeast mixture, both flours, ¾ teaspoon salt, and the butter to form a smooth batter. Let rise at room temperature, covered, until doubled in bulk, about 1 hour.

• Stir the batter smooth. Beat the egg whites until stiff, fold in, and let stand for another 30 minutes.

• Meanwhile, trim the Chinese cabbage and cut into wide strips. Peel the onion and garlic and clean the chili; chop them all.

• First heat the wok and then heat the oil in it. Briefly stir-fry the onion,

garlic, and chili, then stir-fry the Chinese cabbage very quickly. Pour in the broth and cream, and bring to a boil. Season to taste. Remove the mixture and keep warm. Clean the wok.

• Heat the clarified butter in the wok. Fry the batter in portions of 2 tablespoonsful until golden brown, about 2 to 3 minutes. Drain on paper towels and serve with the Chinese cabbage.

Makes 4 servings.

Variation
Use all-purpose flour instead of buckwheat flour; substitute spinach for Chinese cabbage.

PER SERVING:	465 CALORIES
NUTRITIONAL INFORMATION	
Fat (50% calories from fat) 23	g
Protein 9	g
Carbohydrate 44	g
Cholesterol 57	mg
Sodium 89	mg

Spinach Dumplings with Shallot Chutney

Savory • Needs some time

• Cook the potatoes in their skins in salted water. Meanwhile, bring plenty of salted water to the boil. Pick over the spinach and wash thoroughly. Blanch in salted water for about 1 minute. Immediately drain, rinse in ice water, and drain again. Press out all the liquid and chop coarsely. Peel and mince the garlic.

• First heat the wok and then heat 2 tablespoons oil in it. Fry the garlic in the oil until translucent. Add the spinach and braise over medium heat, stirring, 3 to 4 minutes. Remove and set aside.

• Drain the potatoes and peel. While still hot, put them through a ricer into a bowl. Separate the eggs and add the yolks to the potatoes. Mix in the spinach, thyme, cheese, and bread crumbs. Season the mixture well with salt and pepper.

• Peel the shallots and slice lengthwise. Clean the wok. Heat the remaining 2 tablespoons oil in the wok and fry the shallots over medium heat until translucent. Pour in the wine and broth and braise the shallots, covered, until soft, about 5 minutes. Stir in the jelly and season the chutney with salt and pepper. Remove and keep warm. Clean the wok.

• Beat the egg whites until stiff with the baking powder and fold into the spinach dough. Heat the clarified butter in the wok in batches. Using two tablespoons, pull out dumplings from the dough and fry, turning, until golden, about 5 minutes. Drain briefly on paper towels and serve with the shallot chutney.

Makes 4 servings.

---

1 generous pound (500 g) baking potatoes

salt

14 oz (400 g) fresh spinach leaves

1 garlic clove

4 Tbs oil

5 eggs

2 tsp chopped fresh thyme

3½ oz (100 g) Gruyère or Emmentaler cheese, freshly grated

2–3 Tbs bread crumbs

pepper

14 oz (400 g) shallots

7 Tbs red wine or vegetable broth

7 Tbs vegetable broth

3 Tbs red currant jelly

pinch of baking powder

1½–2 cups (12–16 oz/ 375–500 g) clarified butter for deep frying

Preparation time: about 1 hour

PER SERVING:	630 CALORIES	
NUTRITIONAL INFORMATION		
Fat (50% calories from fat) 35		g
Protein 25		g
Carbohydrate 52		g
Cholesterol 427		mg
Sodium 274		mg

Rutabaga Fries

½ small carrot
⅔ cup (5 oz/150 g) bottled curry sauce
2–4 Tbs lemon juice
1 scant cup (7 oz/200 g) heavy cream or crème fraîche
¼ cup (1 oz/30 g) finely chopped mixed fresh herbs
1 tsp Dijon-style mustard
salt
pepper
3½ lb (1.5 kg) rutabagas
2–3 cups (16–24 fl oz/ 500–750 ml) oil for deep frying

Preparation time: about 45 minutes

Rice Rolls

24 spring roll wrappers (rice paper), about 6 in (16 cm) diameter
2 tomatoes
2 oz (60 g) cucumber
3 sprigs dill
½ cup (3 oz/100 g) cooked rice (from about 3 Tbs/1 oz/ 30 g raw; see basic recipe on page 81)
1 egg
2 oz (60 g) Cheddar cheese, freshly grated
salt
pepper
2 egg whites
vegetable oil for frying

Preparation time: about 40 minutes

Rutabaga Fries with Dips

Pictured • Inexpensive

• For the curry dip, peel the carrot and grate fine. Mix with the curry sauce and season to taste with 1 to 2 tablespoons lemon juice. For the herb dip, mix the cream, herbs, and mustard. Season to taste with salt, pepper, and 1 to 2 tablespoons lemon juice.

• Peel the rutabagas, wash, and cut into large pieces. Cut into sticks ¼ in (1 cm) thick and 1½–2 in (4-5 cm) long, using a knife, a mandoline, or the french-fry blade of a food processor.

• First heat the wok and then heat the oil in it. Fry the rutabaga sticks in batches over medium heat until golden brown, 5 to 7 minutes. Drain well. Salt lightly and serve immediately with the dips.

Makes 4 servings.

Variation

Substitute winter squash, pumpkin, or potatoes for rutabaga.

PER SERVING:	507 CALORIES	
NUTRITIONAL INFORMATION		
Fat (55% calories from fat) 32		g
Protein 9		g
Carbohydrate 48		g
Cholesterol 40		mg
Sodium 1531		mg

Little Rice Rolls with Tomatoes and Cheese

Inexpensive • Easy to make

• Lay the wrappers next to each other between damp dish towels until they are soft and pliable, about 10 minutes.

• Meanwhile, scald the tomatoes; peel, halve, and dice them small, removing stem bases and seeds. Wash the cucumbers and dice small. Wash the dill and pick off the tips in coarse pieces. Mix the rice and egg, then mix in the tomatoes, cucumbers, dill, and cheese; season with salt and pepper.

• Put some filling on half of the wrappers. Paint the edges with egg white and lay an unfilled wrapper on top. Fold up one end of the bottom wrapper, fold in the sides, then firmly roll up the package into a cylinder.

• First heat the wok and then heat the oil in it. Fry the rolls in batches until crisp and golden, 3 to 4 minutes. Serve with braised spinach or a vegetable salad.

Makes 4 servings.

PER SERVING:	307 CALORIES	
NUTRITIONAL INFORMATION		
Fat (22% calories from fat) 7		g
Protein 12		g
Carbohydrate 48		g
Cholesterol 88		mg
Sodium 13		mg

Fig Fritters

Elegant • Pictured

• Separate the eggs. Mix the yolks with the wine, flour, sugar, vanilla, lemon peel, and salt to make a smooth, thin batter. Let rest for about 30 minutes. Meanwhile, carefully wash the figs, dry them, and, leaving them unpeeled, quarter them.

• Beat the egg whites stiff and fold into the batter. First heat the wok and then heat the oil in it. Dip the fig quarters into the batter one at a time and fry 2 to 3 minutes or until golden brown.

• Take the fritters out with a skimmer, and drain on paper towels. Serve hot, dusted with powdered sugar. Lemon sherbet or vanilla sauce is an excellent accompaniment.

Makes 4 servings.

Variation

Substitute apricot halves, apple sections, or slices of tropical fruit for the figs.

Summer Rolls with Tropical Fruit

For company • Unusual

• Let the spring roll wrappers thaw. Quarter the banana lengthwise, seed the papaya, peel the pineapple, and dice all the fruit small. Wash the bean sprouts and drain. Wash the herb sprig and cut the leaves into fine strips.

• Heat the wok and then let the butter foam over medium heat. Stir-fry the ginger briefly, then add the sprouts and stir-fry 1 minute. Stir in the fruit and mint and season to taste with lime juice. Remove and set aside. Clean the wok.

• Place 1 to 2 teaspoons filling in the center of half of the wrappers. Paint the edges with egg white and lay an unfilled wrapper on top. Fold up one end of the bottom wrapper, fold in the sides, then firmly roll up the package into a cylinder. Heat the oil in the wok and fry the rolls until golden. Drain on paper towels and serve hot.

Makes 4 servings.

Fig Fritters

2 eggs
1 scant cup (7 fl oz/200 ml) white wine or apple juice
9 Tbs all purpose flour
2 Tbs sugar
½ tsp vanilla extract
1 tsp grated lemon peel
pinch of salt
6 ripe figs
2 cups (16 fl oz/500 ml) oil for deep frying
powdered sugar for dusting

Preparation time: about 45 minutes

Summer Rolls

(for 12 rolls)
24 frozen spring roll wrappers (about 4¼ × 4¼ in/11 × 11 cm)
¼ banana
1 small papaya
about 5 oz (150 g) pineapple
2 oz (60 g) bean sprouts
1 sprig lemon balm or mint
2 tsp butter
1 tsp freshly grated ginger
2 Tbs lime or lemon juice
1 egg white
oil for frying

Preparation time: about 40 minutes

PER SERVING:	330 CALORIES	
NUTRITIONAL INFORMATION		
Fat (39% calories from fat) 13		g
Protein 9		g
Carbohydrate 38		g
Cholesterol 302		mg
Sodium 2		mg

PER SERVING:	328 CALORIES	
NUTRITIONAL INFORMATION		
Fat (23% calories from fat) 8		g
Protein 5		g
Carbohydrate 58		g
Cholesterol 5		mg
Sodium 3		mg

Caressed by Steam

Steaming

In this method, the ingredients are caressed by the hot steam around them without any pressure. Moistness, fresh color, and vitamins—especially in vegetables—are largely preserved, and flavor is accentuated. In addition, steaming minimizes calories because it is accomplished entirely without fat. Sweet yeast dumplings and dough pockets with hearty fillings also like this gentle form of cooking.

Important Helpers

All you need for steaming are two items: the wok with a tightly fitting cover, in which you bring water or some other liquid to a boil, and a sieve attachment or insert on which the food rests and cooks without touching the water. Most woks come with a steamer insert as standard equipment. But you can also use a flexible metal steamer basket insert that fits all wok sizes because its panels can be closed up or opened out. Classically Asian is a bamboo basket with a sieve insert and a cover, of which there may even be several, one piled on top of the other. These are found in various sizes in Asian stores.

If you have no special steamer insert, you can easily improvise one. Lay the ingredients on a plate and set it in the wok on two cups. There must always be enough space between the plate or sieve insert and the sides of the wok so that the steam can rise unimpeded.

Cooking with Steam

Prepare the ingredients according to the recipe and lay them on the sieve insert or on a plate. Pour enough cooking liquid into the wok to just reach the bottom of the steamer but not touch it when boiling. The exact quantity depends on the size of the wok; you'll need 1 to 2 cups (8 to 16 fl oz/250 to 500 ml). Now close the wok with a tight-fitting cover and let the liquid come to a boil over high heat. As soon as steam begins to rise, put the steamer insert or the plate in the wok and immediately cover tightly with the wok cover or basket cover. Turn the heat back to medium and steam the ingredients until done. Do not take off the cover unnecessarily during cooking, or the steam circulation, and thus the cooking process, will be interrupted. But make sure during the cooking time that there is enough liquid in the wok; add some more hot liquid if necessary.

Two Cooking Methods

In "dry steaming" the ingredients are placed directly on the steamer insert, whose small openings immediately bring the rising steam into contact with what is being cooked.

In "wet steaming" the food is first laid on a plate or in a dish and then placed in the steamer basket. This method is used if the ingredients are especially seasoned or marinated and the juices that develop during cooking are to be served.

To Prevent Sticking

Dough pockets or dumplings stick to the steamer basket slightly. To prevent this, brush a metal basket with oil. If you are using a bamboo basket, line it with a few lettuce or vegetable leaves for dough pockets or with a damp cloth napkin for dumplings.

Vegetable Types and Cooking Times

Firm vegetables like potatoes, beets, cauliflower, broccoli, savoy cabbage, carrots, leeks, and peppers are wonderfully suited for steaming. But tender ones like beans and asparagus also do extremely well in a steam bath. (On the other hand, tomatoes, with their high water content, quickly lose their juiciness.) Stuffed vegetables develop a fine flavor. Everything must be very fresh and of top quality, for steaming will reveal any deficiencies in the vegetable's flavor.

Cooking in steam takes somewhat longer than boiling or frying. Precise cooking times are not given in the recipes; they depend on the type of vegetable, its freshness, and the size of the pieces.

Still More Flavor

You can, of course, most easily steam with plain water. But there are two arguments for a flavorful fluid, such as broth or water with a splash of wine or a few fresh herb stalks. First, the flavor of the steam permeates the food and so rounds out its natural flavor. Second, a flavorful base is also created, which you can use for an accompanying sauce or save for making a good soup or for cooking rice.

Allspice, bay leaves, or a piece of lemon peel add a subtle note to the dish. You don't need any fat for steaming. But now and then the taste can be enhanced if the dish is drizzled afterwards with a little melted butter or a flavorful oil such as olive or sesame.

Marinated Leeks

1¾ lb (800 g) thin leeks
½ bunch parsley
7 oz (200 g) mild feta cheese
2 oz (60 g) black olives
1 sprig fresh thyme
5 Tbs cold-pressed olive oil
2 Tbs balsamic vinegar
½ tsp grated lemon peel
1 tsp pink peppercorns

Preparation time:
about 30 minutes

Savoy Cabbage Pouches

salt
12 medium leaves savoy cabbage
2 garlic cloves
2 scallions
1 small carrot
¼ cup (1½ oz/50 g) cooked rice (see basic recipe on page 81)
2 Tbs finely chopped almonds
½ tsp freshly grated ginger
1 tsp grated lemon peel
9 oz (250 g) soft tofu
pepper
light soy sauce

Preparation time:
about 45 minutes

Marinated Leeks

Fast • Easy to make

• Trim the leeks, wash thoroughly, and cut diagonally into pieces about 2 in (5 cm) long. Place in a sieve insert or steamer basket. Add the parsley to 1 to 2 cups (8 to 16 fl oz/250 to 500 ml) water in the wok and bring to a boil. Place the leeks over it and steam, covered, until firm to the bite, about 3 to 5 minutes.

• Meanwhile, cut the cheese into chunks about ¼ in (1 cm) in size. Pit the olives and quarter them. Strip the leaves off the thyme sprig. Beat the oil and vinegar together. Mix the lemon peel, peppercorns, and thyme into the dressing.

• Combine the leeks, feta, and olives in a shallow bowl. Drizzle the dressing over them and toss gently. Let marinate for a short time. Serve with a hearty peasant bread.

Makes 4 servings.

Savoy Cabbage Pouches

Pictured • Inexpensive

• Bring salted water to a boil. Blanch the cabbage leaves in it in batches for about 4 minutes, immediately submerge them in ice water, and allow to drain very well. Peel the garlic and scallions, wash and trim the carrot, and dice all very fine. Mix with the rice. Stir in the almonds, ginger, and lemon peel. Mash the tofu with a fork and knead into the rice mixture; season with salt and pepper. Form mixture into 12 little balls.

• Shave back the thick ribs on the savoy cabbage leaves so they are flat. Set one ball of filling in the middle of each leaf. Form the leaves into little pouches and bind with kitchen string. Set them next to each other in a sieve insert or a steamer basket.

• Bring 1 to 2 cups (8 to 16 fl oz/250 to 500 ml) water to a boil in the wok. Set the cabbage pouches on a rack, and steam, covered, for about 15 minutes. Immediately divide among plates and serve with soy sauce.

Makes 4 servings.

PER SERVING:	306 CALORIES	
NUTRITIONAL INFORMATION		
Fat (61% calories from fat) 22	g
Protein 10	g
Carbohydrate 20	g
Cholesterol 45	mg
Sodium 719	mg

PER SERVING:	100 CALORIES	
NUTRITIONAL INFORMATION		
Fat (34% calories from fat) 4	g
Protein 7	g
Carbohydrate 11	g
Cholesterol 0	mg
Sodium 27	mg

Carrots with Mustard-Basil Sauce

1¾ lb (800 g) carrots with tops
1 bunch basil
½ cup (4 fl oz/100 g) cream
2 Tbs moderately hot mustard
1–2 tsp lemon juice
salt
pepper

Preparation time: about 35 minutes

Broccoli Salad

1¾ lb (800 g) broccoli
1 lemon
1 slice wholewheat toasting bread
1–2 garlic cloves
1½ oz (40 g) peanuts
6 Tbs vegetable broth
5 Tbs olive oil
2 Tbs chopped chives
salt
pepper

Preparation time: about 30 minutes

Carrots with Mustard-Basil Sauce

Decorative • Pictured

• Cut most of the greens off the carrots, leaving about ½ in (2 cm). Peel the carrots, rinse briefly, and halve lengthwise, halving the green as well. Place the carrots in a sieve insert or steamer basket. Wash the basil and pull off the leaves; reserve stems.

• Bring 1 to 2 cups (8 to 16 fl oz/250 to 500 ml) water to a boil in the wok with the basil stems. Place the carrots over it and steam, covered, for 10 to 12 minutes. The carrots should still be crisp.

• In a skillet or wide saucepan, let ¾ cup (6 fl oz/180 ml) of the carrot cooking water and the cream boil until thickened to sauce consistency. Stir in the mustard. Tear up the basil leaves and stir in. Season the sauce to taste with lemon juice, salt, and pepper and serve with the carrots. Also serve roasted potatoes or fried rice.

Makes 4 servings.

PER SERVING:	147 CALORIES
NUTRITIONAL INFORMATION	

Fat (40% calories from fat) 7	g
Protein 3	g
Carbohydrate 20	g
Cholesterol 22	mg
Sodium 166	mg

Warm Broccoli Salad

Fast • Flavorful

• Trim the broccoli, cut into rosettes of equal size, and wash. Peel the stalks and slice. Wash the lemon, grate the peel, and squeeze the juice. Lay the vegetables in a sieve insert or steamer basket. Bring 1 to 2 cups (8 to 16 fl oz/250 to 500 ml) water and the lemon peel to a boil in the wok. Place the broccoli over it and steam, covered, for 7 to 9 minutes (depending on size), until crisp-tender.

• Meanwhile, for the sauce, remove the crusts from the bread. Soften the bread in some water, then squeeze out well. Peel the garlic and puree with the bread, nuts, and broth. Stir in the oil, 1 to 2 teaspoons lemon juice, and the garlic. Season the sauce to taste with salt and pepper.

• In a bowl, mix the broccoli with the sauce and serve warm with pita bread and poached eggs.

Makes 4 servings.

PER SERVING:	230 CALORIES
NUTRITIONAL INFORMATION	

Fat (53% calories from fat) 15	g
Protein 10	g
Carbohydrate 20	g
Cholesterol 0	mg
Sodium 242	mg

Vegetable Plate with Aïoli

From France • Pictured

• Trim the vegetables and wash. Cut the fennel into thin sticks and halve the carrots lengthwise. Quarter the potatoes. Leave the beans whole.

• Bring the broth to a boil in the wok with the thyme. Steam the vegetables in a sieve insert or steamer basket for about 10 minutes; they should retain their crispness. At the same time, hard-boil the eggs.

• Meanwhile, for the aïoli, remove the crusts from the bread. Let the bread soften in the milk for about 5 minutes, and then squeeze out well. Peel the garlic and force through a garlic press into the bread. Mix with the egg yolk to blend well. Beat in the oil little by little until a stiff mayonnaise develops. Stir in the yogurt and season to taste with lemon juice, salt, and pepper.

• Peel the eggs, halve them, and serve with the vegetables. If desired, sprinkle with finely chopped kohlrabi and fennel greens.

Makes 4 servings.

PER SERVING:	549 CALORIES	
NUTRITIONAL INFORMATION		
Fat (61% calories from fat) 38	g
Protein 14	g
Carbohydrate 40	g
Cholesterol 239	mg
Sodium 1018	mg

Zucchini and Mushrooms in Honey Sauce

Exotic • Easy to make

• Trim the zucchini, wash, quarter lengthwise, and cut into pieces about 1 in (3 cm) long. Clean and quarter the mushrooms. Arrange the vegetables decoratively on a round plate (it must be able to fit into the wok!).

• Crumble the chili. Stir together with the broth, both kinds of oil, ginger, cinnamon, honey, orange and lemon juices; season to taste with salt. Drizzle the mixture over the vegetables.

• Bring 1 to 2 cups (8 to 16 fl oz/250 to 500 ml) water to a boil in the wok. Place the vegetable plate on a steamer insert in the wok. Let the vegetables steam, covered, 5 to 7 minutes, or just until tender.

• Meanwhile, roast the sesame seeds in a dry frying pan until fragrant. Trim the scallions and cut into fine rings. Sprinkle both over the vegetables. Serve with rice.

Makes 4 servings.

PER SERVING:	133 CALORIES	
NUTRITIONAL INFORMATION		
Fat (43% calories from fat) 7	g
Protein 5	g
Carbohydrate 16	g
Cholesterol 0	mg
Sodium 184	mg

Vegetable Plate

1 bulb fennel
2 young kohlrabi
9 oz (250 g) slender carrots
2 medium potatoes
9 oz (250 g) green beans
1–2 cups (8–16 fl oz/250–500 ml) vegetable broth
1 sprig thyme
4 eggs
1 slice toasting bread
6 Tbs milk
4–5 garlic cloves
1 egg yolk
½ cup (4 fl oz/125 ml) olive oil
2 Tbs yogurt
lemon juice
salt
pepper

Preparation time: about 35 minutes

Zucchini and Mushrooms

21 oz (600 g) zucchini
7 oz (200 g) fresh button mushrooms
1 dried chili
4 fl oz (125 ml) vegetable broth
2 tsp oil
1 tsp sesame oil
½ tsp freshly grated ginger
pinch of cinnamon
1 tsp honey
5 Tbs orange juice
1 Tbs lemon juice
salt
1 Tbs sesame seeds
2 scallions

Preparation time: about 30 minutes

Yeast Rolls

1 envelope dry yeast
2 tsp sugar
3 cups (14 oz/400 g)
all purpose flour
1 onion
1 garlic clove
1 piece fresh ginger
(about hazelnut size)
1 small carrot
2 sprigs parsley
1 leek
1 Tbs oil
2 Tbs light soy sauce
2 Tbs hoisin sauce
2 tsp sesame oil
salt
pepper
2 Tbs chopped chives

Preparation time: about
2½ hours (of which 1 hour is
resting time)

Stuffed Frying Peppers

21 oz (600 g) mild frying
peppers (long, thin, light-
green peppers)
1–2 garlic cloves
1 bunch dill
½ bunch parsley
2 oz (60 g) pine nuts
10½ oz (300 g) mild feta
cheese
1–2 cups (8–16 fl oz/250–
500 ml) vegetable broth
2–3 Tbs cold-pressed olive oil
pepper

Preparation time:
about 40 minutes

Filled Yeast Rolls

From China • Needs some time

• Dissolve the yeast and 1 teaspoon sugar in ¾ cup (6 fl oz/200 ml) lukewarm water. Add to the flour and knead to make a pliable dough. Let rise, covered, in a warm place for about 1 hour. Then punch down, knead once again, and let rise for another 30 minutes.

• Meanwhile, peel the onion, garlic, and ginger. Wash and trim the carrot, parsley, and leek. Dice all very fine. First heat the wok, then heat the oil in it. Stir-fry the vegetables briefly. Add the soy sauce, hoisin sauce, and 1 teaspoon sesame oil and bring to a boil. Season the filling with the remaining sugar and with salt and pepper.

• Divide the dough into 12 pieces and roll each into a circle about 3 in (8 cm) in diameter. Place some filling in the middle of each, and fold the edges of the dough over it. Bring 1 to 2 cups (8 to 16 fl oz/250 to 500 ml) water to a boil in the wok. Line the steamer insert with a damp cloth, lay the rolls on it, and steam 25 minutes. Serve hot, drizzled with sesame oil and sprinkled with chives.

Makes 4 servings.

PER SERVING:	459 CALORIES	
NUTRITIONAL INFORMATION		
Fat (13% calories from fat) 7	g	
Protein 14	g	
Carbohydrate 86	g	
Cholesterol 1	mg	
Sodium 560	mg	

Stuffed Frying Peppers

From Greece • Pictured

• Slit the peppers lengthwise (or halve them) and carefully seed without removing the stems. Wash and let drain. Peel the garlic. Wash the herbs and chop the leaves fine. Heat the dry wok and roast the pine nuts in it, stirring constantly, until golden.

• Press the liquid out of the cheese with a fork. Force the garlic through a garlic press into it and mix in the pine nuts and herbs. Stuff the pepper cases with the mixture and place them side by side in a sieve insert or steamer basket. Let the vegetable broth come to a boil in the wok and cook the peppers over it, covered, for 7 minutes.

• Arrange the peppers on plates. Drizzle with olive oil and sprinkle with coarsely ground pepper. Mashed potatoes go well with these.

Makes 4 servings.

PER SERVING:	421 CALORIES	
NUTRITIONAL INFORMATION		
Fat (60% calories from fat) 28	g	
Protein 20	g	
Carbohydrate 22	g	
Cholesterol 30	mg	
Sodium 875	mg	

Stuffed Vine Leaves

2 small onions
4 Tbs olive oil
2 oz (60 g) pine nuts
1½ cups (10½ oz/300 g)
cooked long-grain rice
(see basic recipe on page 81)
2 Tbs dried currants
2 Tbs each finely chopped
parsley and dill
1 Tbs finely chopped mint
salt
pepper
16 fresh or bottled vine
leaves
1 bunch chives
2 bay leaves
3–4 Tbs lemon juice

Preparation time:
about 40 minutes

Wontons

7 oz (200 g) frozen spinach
20 frozen wonton wrappers
(4 × 4 in/10 × 10 cm)
4 button mushrooms
2 scallions
2 oz (60 g) canned bamboo
shoots
1 tsp freshly grated ginger
1 garlic clove
1 tsp cornstarch
1–2 tsp sesame oil
pinch of sugar
salt
pepper
a few lettuce leaves

Preparation time:
about 50 minutes

Stuffed Vine Leaves

A new treatment of a classic • For company

• Peel the onions and dice very small. Heat 2 tablespoons oil and fry the onions and pine nuts until golden yellow. Add to the rice with the currants and the herbs. Season with salt and pepper.

• Lay two vine leaves precisely on top of each other, shiny sides down, cutting off the stem ends. Place 1 tablespoonful rice filling on the top leaf, form the leaves into a little sack, and fasten together on top with a chive. Place in a sieve insert or steamer basket. Repeat with the remaining leaves and filling.

• Bring 1 to 2 cups (8 to 16 fl oz/250 to 500 ml) water to a boil in the wok with the bay leaves. Steam the stuffed vine leaves, covered, for 10 minutes. Arrange on a plate and drizzle with the remaining oil and the lemon juice. Warm any leftover filling and serve on the side.

Makes 4 servings.

PER SERVING:	235 CALORIES
NUTRITIONAL INFORMATION	
Fat (41% calories from fat) 11	g
Protein 4	g
Carbohydrate 32	g
Cholesterol 0	mg
Sodium 293	mg

Steamed Wontons

Pictured • Easy to Make

• Thaw the spinach and the wonton wrappers. Squeeze the liquid out of the spinach and chop it fine. Clean the mushrooms and the onions and chop them fine. Drain the bamboo shoots and dice them fine.

• Mix all the chopped ingredients with the ginger; peel the garlic and put it through a garlic press into the mixture. Stir in the cornstarch and 1 teaspoon sesame oil. Season the mixture with sugar, salt, and pepper.

• Put 1 teaspoonful filling in the middle of each wonton wrapper. Holding the wrapper between thumb and forefinger, pull up the dough and pinch it in. There should still be some filling visible in the center.

• Bring 2 to 3 cups (16 to 24 fl oz/480 to 720 ml) water to a boil in the wok. Line a sieve insert or steamer basket with lettuce leaves. Arrange wontons on top and steam, covered, for 10 minutes. Drizzle with the remaining sesame oil.

Makes 4 servings.

PER SERVING:	51 CALORIES
NUTRITIONAL INFORMATION	
Fat (41% calories from fat) 3	g
Protein 2	g
Carbohydrate 6	g
Cholesterol 0	mg
Sodium 42	mg

Vegetables in Cheese Sauce

From Switzerland • Pictured

• Remove the rind from the cheese and grate the cheese coarsely or chop fine. Place in a wide pan with the milk and let stand.

• Bring 1 to 2 cups (8 to 16 fl oz/250 to 500 ml) water to a boil in the wok with the herbs. Trim the vegetables, wash, and cut into pieces of the same size. Place in a sieve insert or steamer basket. Steam the vegetables, covered, until barely cooked, about 10 minutes.

• Meanwhile, melt the cheese in the milk over low heat, stirring constantly. Whisk the wine, lemon juice, cornstarch, and saffron together. Stir into the cheese and bring just to a boil. Season to taste with salt, pepper, and nutmeg.

• Divide the sauce among warmed servings, arrange the vegetables on it, and sprinkle with coarsely ground pepper. Offer potatoes in their skins or bread on the side.

Makes 4 servings.

PER SERVING:	567 CALORIES	
NUTRITIONAL INFORMATION		
Fat (53% calories from fat) 34	g
Protein 34	g
Carbohydrate 32	g
Cholesterol 123	mg
Sodium 921	mg

Asparagus with Carrot Sauce

For company • Delicate

• Peel the carrots and onion and dice them fine. Melt the butter in a saucepan and brown the vegetable cubes over low heat for 3 minutes. Pour in the broth and bring to a boil. Simmer, covered, for 20 minutes.

• Meanwhile, trim and peel the asparagus; place in a sieve insert. Bring 1 to 2 cups (8 to 16 fl oz/250 to 500 ml) water to a boil in the wok. Steam the asparagus, covered, for 10 to 15 minutes (depending on thickness) until it is done but still firm to the bite.

• Dice the cheese. Puree the carrots and onions together with the broth. Let the cheese partially melt in the hot puree. Season the sauce to taste with salt and pepper, sprinkle with chives, and serve with the asparagus. Accompany with potatoes or French bread.

Makes 4 servings.

PER SERVING:	193 CALORIES	
NUTRITIONAL INFORMATION		
Fat (51% calories from fat) 11	g
Protein 10	g
Carbohydrate 15	g
Cholesterol 31	mg
Sodium 890	mg

Vegetables in Cheese Sauce

14 oz (400 g) fontina or raclette cheese
¾ cup (6 fl oz /200 ml) milk
2 tsp herbes de Provence
1¾ lb (800 g) mixed vegetables (e.g., broccoli, bell peppers, leeks, carrots)
5 Tbs dry white wine or milk
2 tsp lemon juice
2 tsp cornstarch
small pinch of saffron
salt
pepper
freshly grated nutmeg

Preparation time: about 35 minutes

Asparagus with Carrot Sauce

1 carrot
1 small onion
1 Tbs butter
⅛ cup (5 fl oz/150 ml) vegetable broth
2½ lb (1.2 kg) white asparagus
3½ oz (100 g) mild blue cheese
salt
pepper
2 Tbs chopped chives

Preparation time: about 45 minutes

Prune Dumplings

From Austria • Pictured

• Melt the butter. Sprinkle the yeast and sugar into the lukewarm milk and let stand until the yeast is dissolved. Mix the yeast mixture into the flour. Add the egg yolk, salt, lemon peel, and melted butter and knead to form a smooth, elastic dough. Let rise, covered, in a warm place for about 15 minutes.

• Flavor the prune filling with cinnamon and rum. Divide the dough into 12 pieces and press each flat in the palm of your hand. Fill with some prune mixture, and form into a dumpling. Let rise about 15 minutes.

• Bring 1 to 2 cups (8 to 16 fl oz/250 to 500 ml) water to a boil in the wok. Line a steamer basket or sieve insert with a damp cloth. Set the dumplings on it next to each other and steam, covered, for 15 to 20 minutes. To serve, sprinkle with poppy seeds and powdered sugar, and drizzle with hot melted butter.

Makes 4 servings.

PER SERVING:	432 CALORIES	
NUTRITIONAL INFORMATION		
Fat (44% calories from fat) 21		g
Protein 10		g
Carbohydrate 51		g
Cholesterol 91		mg
Sodium 149		mg

Filled Cottage Cheese Pockets

For children • Inexpensive

• Puree the cottage cheese in a blender or food processor, or force it through a sieve.

• Wash the potatoes and boil 15 to 20 minutes until soft. Peel and mash or put them through a food mill while still hot. Let cool. Knead the mashed potatoes to a smooth dough with the butter, flour, semolina, salt, and egg yolk.

• Roll out the dough ⅛ in (.5 cm) thick on a lightly floured work surface. Cut out circles about 3 in (8 cm) in diameter.

• For the filling, stir together the cottage cheese, vanilla sugar, and berries. Fill each dough circle with the mixture, fold it over, and press the edges together.

• Bring 1 to 2 cups (8 to 16 fl oz/250 to 500 ml) water to a boil in the wok. Grease a sieve insert and arrange the pockets in it. Steam for 10 minutes. Serve with bread crumbs browned in butter and pear compote.

Makes 4 servings.

PER SERVING:	280 CALORIES	
NUTRITIONAL INFORMATION		
Fat (25% calories from fat) 8		g
Protein 9		g
Carbohydrate 45		g
Cholesterol 64		mg
Sodium 53		mg

Prune Dumplings

1 Tbs butter
1⅔ cups (7 oz/200 g) all-purpose flour
½ envelope dry yeast
1 Tbs sugar
5 Tbs lukewarm milk
1 egg yolk
pinch of salt
1 tsp grated lemon peel
3½ oz (100 g) prune pastry filling (lekvar)
¼ tsp cinnamon
1 tsp rum (optional)
1¾ oz (50 g) ground poppy seeds
powdered sugar for dusting
3 Tbs butter for drizzling

Preparation time: about 1¼ hours (of which 30 minutes is rising time)

Filled Cottage Cheese Pockets

½ cup (4 oz/120 g) dry-curd cottage cheese
14 oz (400 g) baking potatoes
1½ Tbs soft butter
¾ cup (3½ oz/100 g) all-purpose flour
2 Tbs semolina, farina, or Cream of Wheat
pinch of salt
1 egg yolk
flour for work surface
1 packet vanilla sugar
3 oz (90 g) fresh or frozen blueberries
oil

Preparation time: about 1½ hours (of which 30 minutes is cooling time)

everyone is
wokking

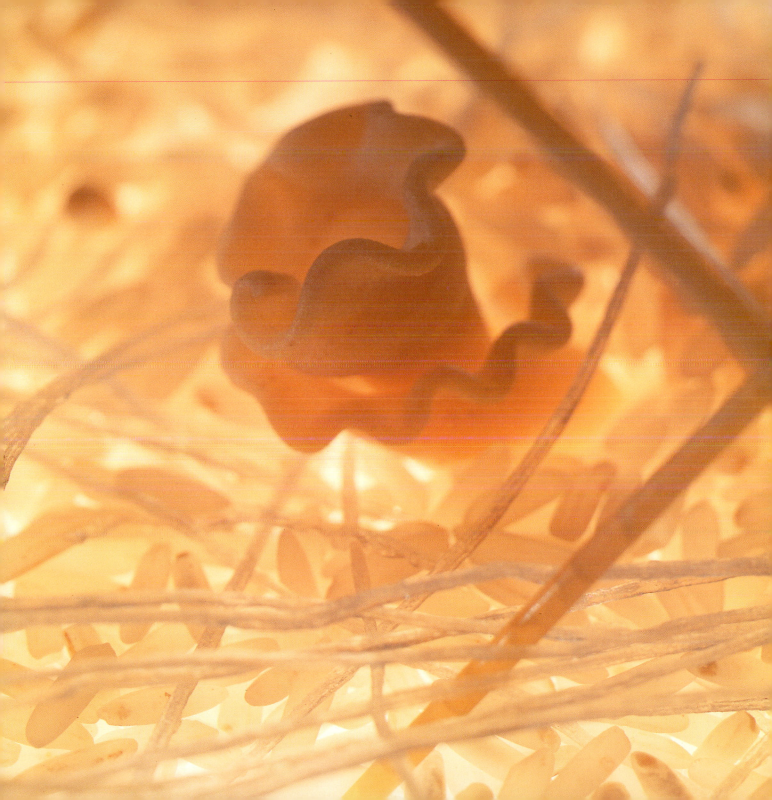

Noodles and Rice

To this day no one is certain whether the Chinese or the Italians invented the noodle, or whether it was invented more or less at the same time in entirely different regions of the world. But one thing is certain: Asians are just as passionate noodle lovers as Westerners, and they are familiar with just as many variations. In Asia, noodles bring luck and promise health, well-being, and a long life. No wonder, then, that there are so many noodle recipes in the Far Eastern cuisines—and most of them are prepared in the wok.

Rice ranks even higher than noodles, serving as the focus of most Asian meals. Thus the Far East also offers innumerable ideas for conjuring up quick and delicious dishes in the wok out of cooked rice and a few fresh ingredients. But Western noodle and rice dishes prepared in the wok have a charm of their own.

International Noodle Varieties

In the West they are usually divided as follows:

• Durum wheat noodles consist entirely of durum semolina and water. They are recognizable by their light yellow, almost transparent color and smooth surface.

• Egg noodles are produced from durum wheat, soft wheat, or a mixture of both and eggs.

• Whole-grain noodles contain flour made from the entire kernel, including the germ and the outer husk (bran). Among them are those made of rye, wheat, millet, and soybeans. They are produced with or without eggs.

Of the Asian noodle varieties, the following are available in North America:

• Rice noodles consist of rice flour and water. When raw they look almost transparent but they become snow-white with cooking.

• Transparent noodles are very thin, glassy-looking noodles made of mung bean starch and water. They also remain transparent when cooked.

• Wheat noodles are produced of eggs and wheat flour. They are available as long spaghetti or ribbon noodles in several widths. Often they are pressed into practical little packets.

• Buckwheat noodles are somewhat thicker than our spaghetti; they play an important role in Japanese cooking.

Rice Without Borders

Rice is a main source of nutrition for half the world's people. About 8,000 varieties are cultivated around the globe. These are the best known:

• Patna rice is a common long-grain variety that is especially fluffy, with separate grains, when cooked.

• Basmati, originally from India, is counted among the most elegant and also most expensive polished long-grained varieties. It gives off an incomparable fragrance when cooking and has a fine flavor. Its name means "the fragrant one."

• Fragrant rice comes mainly from Thailand and China. It is similar to Basmati, with firm, separate grains, and is very flavorful.

• Glutinous rice also grows in Asia. It has a very high starch content and is a medium-grain rice; the cooked grains stick gently to each other and can be picked up with chopsticks particularly easily.

• Arborio, an Italian medium-grain rice, is the most popular risotto rice because it can take up much liquid.

• Wild rice is really not a rice but the grain of a water grass that is native to the United States and Canada. The long, black-brown grains have a delicious, nutty taste but are quite expensive. Wild rice can also be bought mixed with other kinds of rice.

Cooking Rice Perfectly

In Asia the preferred way to cook rice is in a rice cooker, which is child's play to use and produces perfect results. Now these are also available in the West, in Asian stores and well-stocked housewares stores. But even without one of these technical aids, rice cooking is quite simple: For 4 people, use 1¼ cups (9 oz/250 g) raw rice. If the package so instructs, wash the rice in a sieve under running water until the water runs clear. (Domestically grown rice is enriched with a surface coating of B vitamins and should not be rinsed.) Put the rice in a wok or other wide, thick-walled pot and add enough water to rise barely two fingers high over its surface. Salt lightly and bring to a boil without the cover; then let the rice simmer, covered, over low heat for about 20 minutes or until the liquid has been absorbed.

Tip

Figure that 9 oz (250 g) raw rice gives 26 to 27 oz (750 g) cooked rice (about three times the amount). For dishes using cooked rice, let the rice cool completely, uncovered, preferably letting it stand overnight. Then fluff it up a little.

81

Pasta

*7 oz (200 g) pasta
(e.g., tagliatelle)
salt
2 small red onions
10 oz (300 g) radicchio
1 bunch arugula (about
3½ oz/100 g)
¼ cup (2 fl oz/60 ml) olive oil
¼ cup (2 fl oz/60 ml) red wine
or vegetable broth
pepper*

*Preparation time:
about 25 minutes*

Rice Noodles

*9 oz (250 g) Asian rice
noodles
2 garlic cloves
1 piece fresh ginger (about
½ in/2 cm)
1 fresh red chili
1 green bell pepper
2 medium zucchini
2 stalks celery
3–4 scallions
4 stalks cilantro
4–5 Tbs oil
3 Tbs vegetable broth
4–5 Tbs light soy sauce
2 Tbs mild white wine
vinegar
pinch of sugar
pepper*

*Preparation time:
about 30 minutes*

Pasta with Radicchio

Fast • Pictured

• Cook the pasta in plenty of boiling salted water according to directions for al dente.

• Meanwhile, peel the onions and chop coarsely. Trim and wash the radicchio and the arugula; cut the radicchio into narrow strips, the arugula into broad ones.

• First heat the wok, then heat the oil in it. Fry the onions until transparent, stirring. Pour in the wine and let simmer for about 2 minutes. Fold in the radicchio and fry for about 1 minute; season with salt and pepper.

• Drain the pasta and add to the wok. Heat, stirring. At the end, stir in the arugula and season the pasta to taste with salt and pepper.

Makes 4 servings.

Rice Noodles with Green Vegetables

Fast • Easy to make

• Soften the rice noodles in lukewarm water for about 10 minutes.

• Meanwhile, peel the garlic and ginger and mince very fine. Wash the chili pepper, clean, and chop fine. Wash the vegetables, clean, and cut into bite-sized pieces. Wash the cilantro and pull the leaves from the stems.

• Drain the noodles and cut into pieces about 4 in (10 cm) long. First heat the wok, then heat the oil in it. Briefly stir-fry the garlic, ginger, and chili. Then stir-fry the vegetables for about 3 minutes, adding the broth little by little.

• Stir in the rice noodles and fry all together for about 2 minutes. Season the dish to taste with soy sauce, vinegar, sugar, and pepper. Fold in the cilantro.

Makes 4 servings.

PER SERVING:	335 CALORIES
NUTRITIONAL INFORMATION	
Fat (24% calories from fat) 9	g
Protein 9	g
Carbohydrate 53	g
Cholesterol 0	mg
Sodium 20	mg

PER SERVING:	421 CALORIES
NUTRITIONAL INFORMATION	
Fat (30% calories from fat) 15	g
Protein 8	g
Carbohydrate 70	g
Cholesterol 1	mg
Sodium 1387	mg

7 oz (200 g) transparent noodles
1 Tbs dried cloud ear mushrooms
2 Tbs sesame seeds
2 eggs
4–5 Tbs light soy sauce
4 tsp sesame oil
sugar
salt
pepper
4–5 Tbs oil
7 oz (200 g) carrots
5 oz (150 g) canned bamboo shoots
7 oz (200 g) leeks
7 oz (200 g) spinach
3 oz (100 g) bean sprouts
2 onions
2 garlic cloves
2 dried chilis

Preparation time: about 50 minutes

Transparent Noodles with Vegetables

From Korea • Easy to make

• Pour boiling water over the transparent noodles and the mushrooms (separately) and let soften for about 30 minutes.

• Meanwhile, heat the dry wok and roast the sesame seeds, stirring constantly, until fragrant. Remove and set aside. Stir the eggs together with 1 tablespoon soy sauce, 1 teaspoon sesame oil, a pinch of sugar, and some salt and pepper. Heat 2 tablespoons oil in the wok. Make two omelets with the egg mixture over low heat. Remove them and set aside, covered.

• Wash and trim the vegetables. Cut the carrots and drained bamboo shoots into matchsticks. Cut the leeks into rings, the spinach into strips. Peel the onions and garlic. Cut the onion into rings and mince the garlic. Crumble the chilis.

• Drain the transparent noodles and cut them into shorter pieces with scissors. Rinse the mushrooms, remove the tough parts, and cut the mushrooms into strips. Roll up the omelets and cut into fine strips.

• Heat 1 tablespoon oil in the wok at a time. Fry the vegetables and mushrooms in two to three batches over high heat, stirring constantly and seasoning with salt, pepper, some sugar, and soy sauce.

• Put all the vegetables, mushrooms, noodles, roasted sesame seeds, and remaining sesame oil in the wok and heat, stirring constantly. Season to taste with salt, pepper, and soy sauce. Carefully fold in the omelet strips at the end.

Makes 4 servings.

PER SERVING:	459 CALORIES
NUTRITIONAL INFORMATION	

Fat (37% calories from fat) 19	g
Protein 15	g
Carbohydrate 59	g
Cholesterol 90	mg
Sodium 2314	mg

Saffron-Vegetable Rice

1¾ oz (50 g) cashew nuts
1 cinnamon stick
6 cardamom seeds
4 cloves
2 bay leaves
1 carrot
pinch of saffron
2 Tbs clarified butter
1¼ cups (9 oz/250 g) Basmati rice
1 Tbs raisins
5 oz (150 g) frozen peas
2 cups (16 fl oz/500 ml) vegetable broth
salt
1 tsp sugar
1 handful spinach leaves
pepper

Preparation time:
about 35 minutes

Leek-Pineapple Rice

10 oz (300 g) leeks
1 lb (450 g) pineapple
3 Tbs oil
1 Tbs curry powder
1 cup (8 fl oz/250 ml) vegetable broth
pinch of sugar
3 cups (24 oz/600 g) cooked rice (see basic recipe on page 81)
salt

Preparation time:
about 30 minutes

Saffron-Vegetable Rice

From India • Pictured

• Coarsely chop the cashews. Roast the nuts and spices one after the other in the dry wok until fragrant. Remove and set aside. Peel the carrot and dice it small. Dissolve the saffron in 2 tablespoons hot water.

• Heat the clarified butter in the wok. Fry the carrot and rice in it briefly. Add the nuts, spices, bay leaves, raisins, peas, and saffron and fry together. Deglaze the wok with the broth and season with salt and sugar. Let all come to a boil and cook over low heat, covered, for 10 minutes.

• Meanwhile, pick over the spinach, wash it, and cut it into wide strips. Stir the spinach into the wok and cook for about 10 more minutes or until the rice is soft and all the liquid has been absorbed. Season with salt and pepper.

Makes 4 servings.

Leek-Pineapple Rice

Fast • Hot

• Trim the leeks, wash thoroughly, and cut into diagonal pieces about ½ in (1.5 cm) long. Peel and dice the pineapple.

• Heat the wok and then heat the oil in it. Stir-fry the leeks for 3 minutes. Dust with curry powder and brown briefly. Add the broth and sugar and boil over high heat for 2 minutes.

• Add the rice and pineapple to the wok and heat through, stirring. Season with salt to taste.

Makes 4 servings.

PER SERVING:	509 CALORIES
NUTRITIONAL INFORMATION	
Fat (27% calories from fat) . . . . 16 g	
Protein . . . . 13 g	
Carbohydrate . . . . 82 g	
Cholesterol . . . . 19 mg	
Sodium . . . . 893 mg	

PER SERVING:	277 CALORIES
NUTRITIONAL INFORMATION	
Fat (24% calories from fat) . . . . 8 g	
Protein . . . . 5 g	
Carbohydrate . . . . 48 g	
Cholesterol . . . . 0 mg	
Sodium . . . . 135 mg	

Chinese Fried Rice

Fast • Inexpensive

• Wash and trim all the vegetables. Peel the carrot, onion, garlic, and ginger and dice very fine. Cut the scallions into rings and the pepper into strips.

• First heat the wok and then 1 teaspoon each of both kinds of oils in it. Stir the eggs with 1 tablespoon soy sauce, pour into the wok, and scramble just until firm. Remove and keep warm. Clean the wok.

• Heat the remaining oil in the wok. Stir in the carrot, onion, garlic, and ginger; add the pepper and sprouts. Stir-fry all over high heat for about 2 minutes; add salt and pepper.

• Add the rice and scallions and stir-fry until everything is hot. Loosely fold in the scrambled egg, season the rice with the remaining soy sauce, drizzle the broth over it, and season to taste with lemon juice. Fold in the cilantro.

Makes 4 servings.

PER SERVING:	423 CALORIES	
NUTRITIONAL INFORMATION		
Fat (31% calories from fat) 16		g
Protein 17		g
Carbohydrate 60		g
Cholesterol 236		mg
Sodium 856		mg

Chickpea Rice

Oriental • Subtle

• The night before, soften the chickpeas by covering them with water. The next day let them simmer in the soaking water, covered, for about 30 minutes.

• Meanwhile, wash and trim the vegetables. Slice the white part of the scallions thinly and cut the green part into pieces about 1 in (3 cm) long. Dice the zucchini. Drain the chickpeas, reserving the water.

• First heat the wok and then heat the oil in it. Stir-fry the green scallion sections and the zucchini. Remove and season with salt and pepper. Stir-fry the white scallion slices until transparent. Season with salt, pepper, and paprika.

• Bring the chickpeas, rice, and 2 cups (16 fl oz/500 ml) of the cooking water to a boil in the wok and simmer, covered, over low heat for 25 minutes. Add the onions and zucchini and heat through. Season to taste, sprinkle with herbs, and drizzle with lemon juice to taste.

Makes 4 servings.

PER SERVING:	601 CALORIES	
NUTRITIONAL INFORMATION		
Fat (15% calories from fat) 11		g
Protein 21		g
Carbohydrate 113		g
Cholesterol 0		mg
Sodium 228		mg

Cabbage Noodles

12 oz (350 g) cabbage
1 onion
10 oz (300 g) ribbon noodles
salt
2 Tbs oil
1 tsp sugar
3 Tbs vegetable broth
1 tsp caraway seeds
pepper
paprika

Preparation time:
about 35 minutes

Carrot Rice

1¼ lbs (600 g) carrots
salt
2–3 garlic cloves
2 Tbs fresh rosemary
7 oz (200 g) Gorgonzola or other blue cheese
¼ cup (2 fl oz/60 ml) olive oil
26 oz (750 g) cooked wild rice mixture (9 oz/250 g raw, see basic recipe on page 81)
black pepper
¼ cup (1 oz/30 g) sliced hazelnuts or almonds

Preparation time:
about 30 minutes

Austrian Cabbage Noodles

Economical • Easy to make

• Wash the cabbage and cut into short, narrow strips. Peel the onion and chop. Cook the noodles in salted water according to the package directions for al dente.

• Meanwhile, first heat the wok and then heat the oil in it. Let the sugar caramelize in the oil. Stir in the onion and fry until bright yellow. Add the cabbage and broth to the wok, season with caraway, salt, and pepper, and steam the cabbage over low heat, stirring occasionally, until soft, about 15 minutes.

• Drain the noodles. Add to the wok and cook 5 minutes longer. Season to taste and dust with paprika.

Makes 4 servings.

PER SERVING:	352 CALORIES
NUTRITIONAL INFORMATION	
Fat (18% calories from fat) 7	g
Protein 12	g
Carbohydrate 60	g
Cholesterol 71	mg
Sodium 249	mg

Fried Carrot Rice

Fast • Pictured

• Clean the carrots and use a peeler to cut lengthwise into thin slices. Meanwhile, bring a pot of salted water to boil. Blanch the carrots in it for 3 minutes, then plunge into ice water and drain well.

• Peel the garlic and cut it into paper-thin slices. Chop the rosemary fine. Cut the Gorgonzola into small cubes.

• First heat the wok and then heat the oil in it. Stir-fry the carrots and garlic for 3 minutes. Add the rice and rosemary and stir-fry another 3 to 4 minutes. Add salt and pepper.

• Fold in the cheese cubes and sprinkle the nuts over the rice.

Makes 4 servings.

PER SERVING:	553 CALORIES
NUTRITIONAL INFORMATION	
Fat (41% calories from fat) 26	g
Protein 21	g
Carbohydrate 63	g
Cholesterol 0	mg
Sodium 52	mg

Rice Pudding

2 cups (16 fl oz/500 ml) milk
⅔ cup (4 oz /125 g) short-grain rice
pinch of salt
2 Tbs sugar
1½ oz (40 g) each, candied orange and lemon peel
2 oz (60 g) chopped almonds
2 Tbs chopped pistachios
2 Tbs butter
1 lemon
2 Tbs raisins
2 Tbs orange liqueur (optional)
mint leaves for garnish

Preparation time:
about 35 minutes

Lime Noodles

5 oz (150 g) ribbon noodles
salt
2 limes
7 oz (200 g) tomatillos
1 Tbs butter
1 tsp freshly grated ginger
2 Tbs sugar
½ cup (4 fl oz/125 g) cream

Preparation time:
about 25 minutes

Oriental Rice Pudding

Easy to make • Delicate

• In a saucepan combine the milk, rice, salt, and sugar and bring to a boil. Reduce heat to low and let simmer, covered, for 20 minutes. Meanwhile, chop the orange and lemon peels fine.

• Heat the dry wok over medium heat. Add the almonds and pistachios and roast, stirring, until fragrant. Remove and set aside.

• Melt the butter in the wok. Add the cooked rice, and stir-fry 2 to 3 minutes. Wash the lemon under hot water, grate the peel, and squeeze the juice. Mix the lemon and orange peels, almonds, pistachios, grated lemon peel, raisins, and liqueur into the rice. Season to taste with lemon juice. To serve, garnish with mint leaves. A good accompaniment is store-bought or homemade apricot or orange sauce.

Makes 4 servings.

Variation

Mix finely chopped fresh fruit into the finished rice.

PER SERVING:	413 CALORIES	
NUTRITIONAL INFORMATION		
Fat (40% calories from fat) 11		g
Protein 8		g
Carbohydrate 29		g
Cholesterol 21		mg
Sodium 2		mg

Lime Noodles with Tomatillos

Zesty • Pictured

• Cook the noodles al dente according to package directions.

• Wash the limes under hot water, dry, and remove the skin in thin strips with a zester. Squeeze out the juice. Carefully loosen the tomatillos from their husks, wash, and cut in half.

• First heat the wok and then melt the butter in it. Briefly stir-fry the ginger. Stir in the sugar and lime juice, and finally pour in the cream.

• Drain the noodles. Heat with the tomatillos and half the lime peel in the sauce, stirring occasionally. Sprinkle with the remaining lime peel.

Makes 4 servings.

Variation

Stir in 2 to 3 tablespoons orange liqueur with the cream.

PER SERVING:	282 CALORIES	
NUTRITIONAL INFORMATION		
Fat (40% calories from fat) 11		g
Protein 6		g
Carbohydrate 33		g
Cholesterol 35		mg
Sodium 42		mg

INDEX

See the inside front cover for Preparing Vegetables for Wok Cooking, and see the inside back cover for Cutting Techniques.

IMPRINT

Published originally under the title
Vegetarisches Im Wok

© 1997 by Gräfe and Unzer Verlag
GmbH, München

English translation © Copyright
1998 by Barron's Educational
Series, Inc.

German edition by Marlisa
Szwillus, Photography by
Heinz-Josef Beckers
English translation by Elizabeth
D. Crawford

*All inquiries should be
addressed to:*
Barron's Educational Series, Inc.
250 Wireless Boulevard
Hauppauge, NY 11788
http://www.barronseduc.com

Library of Congress Catalog
Card No. 98-22860

International Standard Book
No. 0-7641-0689-9

**Library of Congress Cataloging-
in-Publication Data**
Szwillus, Marlisa.
  [Vegetarisches im Wok. English]
  Vegetarian wok cooking /
Marlisa Szwillus ; English
translation by Elizabeth D.
Crawford ; photography by Heinz-
Josef Beckers.
    p. cm.
  Includes index.
  ISBN 0-7641-0689-9
  1. Vegetarian cookery. 2. Wok
cookery.   I. Title.
TX837.S9913   1998
641.5′636—dc21   98-22860
                         CIP

Printed in Hong Kong

9 8 7 6 5 4 3 2 1

Acknowledgments:
Josh Westrich and Christoph Fein
for their collaboration in the
creation of the photographs in
their photo studio in Essen,
Germany.

Marlisa Szwillus developed her
love for cooking at a very young
age, for her parents placed great
value on good food and ingredients of the highest quality. This
led to her joy in cooking and eat-
ing. Her career as a freelance food
journalist and cookbook author
sprang from her study of organic
nutrition, her position as a food
editor for a well-known woman's
magazine, and director of the culi-
nary department of the largest
German food and home magazine
for several years.

Heinz-Josef Beckers studied com-
munications design at the Univer-
sity of Essen GHS (Folkwang). He
maintains a studio for photography and design in the vicinity of
Frankfurt am Main. Food, still
lifes, and experimental photography are among his areas of spe-
cialization, along with conceptual
and graphic work for industry,
publishers, and agencies.

The Perfect Cut

Cooking in a wok is easy and fast because all the ingredients are already cut into small pieces. In China the vegetables are chopped with masterly precision so that everything cooks evenly, the flavors are optimally blended and, of course, the greatest possible delight to the eye is created. To achieve this, it is important to use the correct chopping technique. Each vegetable has a particular character, whether it is a root, leaf, or fruit, either tender or firm. Basically, the more delicate the structure of the ingredient (for example, mushrooms, zucchini, and leek), the larger the pieces may be. If the structure is firm (like that of potatoes and other root vegetables), the pieces must be somewhat smaller.

Good Kitchen Tools
You can only do perfect (and, with practice, also fast) chopping with a large, sharp knife with a broad blade. Good knives are not cheap, but the same thing goes for knives as for pots and pans: Quality pays.

You can also chop vegetables with a Chinese cleaver. With this tool you can get results ranging from coarse chopping to filigree-fine strips. Also required is a large cutting board, which must rest on the work surface with absolutely no chance of slipping.

Cutting Technique: Slicing
All slices must be as close to the same thickness as possible. Slanted slices look particularly attractive. With firm vegetables like carrots, celery root, kohlrabi, or cucumbers, this works out best on a vegetable slicer or mandoline. As necessary, large slices can then be cut into fork- or chopstick-ready size. With mushrooms, the stems are removed first and then the top is sliced crosswise. Seasonings like garlic and ginger are generally cut into paper-thin slices.